Appliqué Innovations

MACHINE TECHNIQUES FOR BEAUTIFUL CLOTHING

By Agnes Mercik

Appliqué Innovations

MACHINE TECHNIQUES FOR BEAUTIFUL CLOTHING

By Agnes Mercik

Sterling Publishing Co., Inc.
New York

A Sterling/Sewing Information Resources Book

Sewing Information Resources

Owner: JoAnn Pugh-Gannon

Photography: Kaz Ayukawa, K Graphics

Book Design & Layout: Rose Sheifer, Graphic Productions, Walnut Creek, California

Index: Anne Leach

Library of Congress Cataloging-in-Publication Data
Mercik, Agnes
      Applique innovations : machine techniques for beautiful clothing / by Agnes Mercik.
         p.   cm.
      "A Sterling/Sewing Information Resources Book."
      Includes index.
      ISBN 0-8069-0355-4
      1. Machine appliqué. 2. Clothing and dress. I. title.
TT779.M47   1997
746.44'5—dc21   97-12796
                                              CIP

Published by Sterling Publishing Company, Inc.
387 Park Avenue South, New York, N.Y. 10016
Produced by Sewing Information Resources
P.O. Box 330, Wasco, Il. 60183
©1997 by Agnes Mercik
Distributed in Canada by Sterling Publishing
c/o Canadian Manda Group, One Atlantic Avenue, Suite 105
Toronto, Ontario, Canada, M6K 3E7
Distributed in Great Britain and Europe by Cassell PLC
Wellington House, 125 Strand, London WC2R 0BB, England
Distributed in Australia by Capricorn Link (Australia) Pty Ltd.
P.O. Box 6651, Baulkham Hills, Business Centre, NSW 2153, Australia

Printed in United States
2 4 6 8 10 9 7 5 3 1

Sterling ISBN 0-8069-0355-4

DEDICATION

There are many people who, on both a personal and professional basis, were in some way involved in bringing this book to completion.

I wish to dedicate this book to all the creative people, students, and associates in the sewing industry who have continued to encourage and give me their endless support through their friendships.

After continually being asked, "When are you going to write another book?" I can finally say "Here it is!"

ACKNOWLEDGMENTS

I want to thank my parents for teaching me the value of working hard in order to attain my goals.

My appreciation and thanks further extend to:

JoAnn Pugh-Gannon for her patient and professional guidance and compassion in taking this book project from conception to completion.

Gayle Hillert, for additional support, and **Bernina of America** for the loan of dependable sewing equipment, such as sewing and overlock machines, the Deco™ embroidery machine, a Bernette™ iron, and unlimited amount of machine accessories.

Newman Sewing Machines for their thorough and efficient service in helping me keep all my sewing equipment working in top form at all times.

Nancy Farrell for her professional sewing expertise in completing sample garments.

To my family — my sons, daughter-in-law, and grandchildren — and friends, who are like family, for their special encouragement and services throughout the book gestation process.

Last but not least, **to my husband, Hank,** my wonderful companion, best friend, and understanding confidant, for his patience in putting up with a "creative mess" that extended beyond my sewing studio room. His added responsibilities of adviser, travel agent, chauffeur, porter, secretary, and cook helped me tremendously to keep my mind focused on this book.

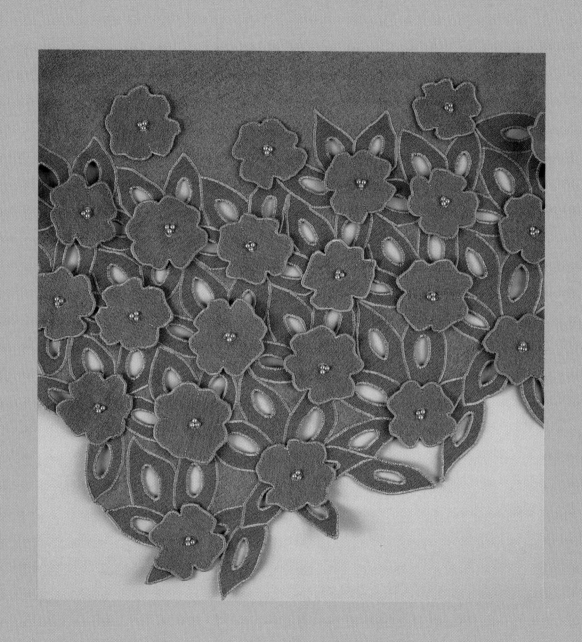

THANK YOU

A special thank you is extended to the following companies for their generous help, use of products and support of this book:

- ❖ Bernina of America (Sewing machines, overlocks, accessories, and irons)

- ❖ Capitol Imports (Fabric, and lace)

- ❖ Kwik Sew; Park Bench Pattern Co.; and Great Copy Patterns (Patterns).

- ❖ June Tailor (Pressing materials, cutting equipment).

- ❖ Coats & Clark; KIC2 (formerly Rainbow Elastic); Rhode Island Textile Co.; SCS - USA Madeira; Madeira USA Ltd.; Sew Art International; Speed Stitch; and YLI Corporation (Threads, and stabilizers).

- ❖ Dritz Corporation and Handler Textile Corporation (Interfacings, and stabilizers).

The following retailers were also very generous with their time and assistance:

A Different Touch, Virginia Beach, VA; Ann's Fabrics, Canton, MA; Bernina Sewing Center, Tuscon AZ; Fabric Gallery, Cheshire, CT; Fabric Studio, Swansea, MA; Gina's Sewing Center, Knoxville, TN; Gloversville Sewing Center, Gloversville, NY; Mulberry Silks, Carrboro, NC; Newman Sewing Machines, Springfield, MA; Sewing Gallery, Augusta, GA; and The Silver Thimble, Havre, MT (Fabrics, buttons, notions, and patterns).

TABLE OF CONTENTS

INTRODUCTION

Appliqué has been a popular embroidery technique for many centuries and continues to be one of my favorite machine-art expressions. This topic is so vast and the variations so numerous that it would take more than one book to cover all of its unusual and interesting aspects. Shaped fabrics can be layered on top of the base fabric or behind, then cut away and stitched; or a separate piece of fabric can be stitched for a three-dimensional form, then partially attached to the base motif.

Stitching can be done on top of the fabric with needle threads enhancing the motif or stitched from behind on the wrong side using thicker bobbin threads highlighting the right side.

The fabric might be scrunched, punched, dyed, and manipulated beyond original recognition. It also could be unraveled with individual fabric threads wound in the bobbin and then stitched back onto the original fabric creating still another type of texture.

We also can create our own "fabric" by stitching a variety of threads onto a stabilizer. After sufficient stitching, the stabilizer is then removed and the thread becomes a sheer fabric.

I have added the cover stitch and the two-thread chain stitch of my sergers to this technique which adds another dimension and also speeds up the process.

Then there is the "appliqué-less" technique where a piece of fabric is not used for the motif. The outline of the design is merely stitched onto the fabric for still another adaptation. I have partnered this technique with its traditional counterpart to create interesting texture combinations.

STARTING WITH THE NECESSITIES

What Is Appliqué?

Appliqué, in its simplest form, is a decorative sewing technique described as applying single or multiple pieces of fabrics or material to a base fabric. These pieces of material, called motifs, are first fused onto the project and then stitched by hand or machine, the latter of which is considered the fastest, easiest, and most creative method of application.

It also can be considered a form of machine thread painting, as the motifs can be stitched to the base fabric using a variety of thread colors and textures. The effect can be tone-on-tone, subtle varying shades of one color, or a bold and exciting contrast of colors and metallic threads.

This technique can be simple, elaborate, or used in combination with other sewing methods and decorative additions. Embellishments, such as beads, sequins, semi-precious stones, and unusual thicknesses and textures of cords and yarns, can be couched onto or around the motifs for added interest.

There are numerous means of stitching the motifs to the base fabric, such as straight stitching, automatic utility and decorative stitching, free-motion stitching, decorative bobbin stitching, and satin stitching, which is the most common method. Creatively the only thing stopping you is your imagination.

All About Fabrics

Almost any type of fabric can be used as the base for a garment or project along with any combination of fabrics in the same appliqué design. However, the main criteria to keep in mind for final use where machine washing or dry cleaning are concerned is that all the fabrics used in one project be compatible. Since some fabrics shrink or release dyes, pre-treating is recommended. Some lames and fine or loosely woven fabrics usually require additional stabilization. Use the finest fusible tricot available for this purpose.

Though light- to medium-weight, smooth-surfaced, woven fabrics are the easiest to handle, your creativity is enhanced when you use a variety of fabric combinations. Some fabric suggestions for appliqué are sheers, knits, lace, and metallic fabrics and nonwoven fabrics such as Ultrasuede™, Ultraleather™, natural reptile and animal skins, suede, and leather.

For elegant tone-on-tone variations, use the same fabric on the right or wrong side. Before cutting out the motifs, study the grainline of the fabric for each piece. When stitched on the same background fabric, shifting the grainline direction lends a subtle effect to the overall design.

Look for fabrics with unusual textures and abstract designs, those that have been dyed with color gradations, and ones that are, simply stated, just interesting.

Since every fabric has its own desirable and particular properties, each requires its own approach regarding stabilizers, needles, and specific machine adjustments.

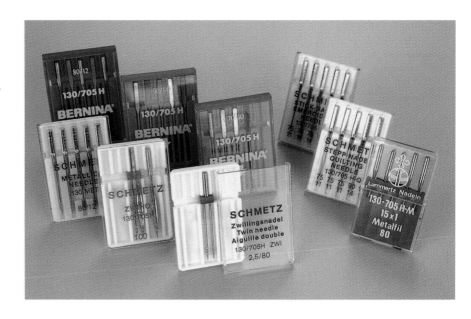

Needles

The correct needle use is the key to sewing and serging success. Choosing the proper needle for each project deserves your special attention. Guidelines, such as starting each project with a new needle and selecting and inserting the correct needle, size, and design according to the fabric and thread you are using, combine to ensure successful sewing and serging results.

With the continuing introduction of new types of fibers in fabrics along with a variety of new textured threads and yarns entering the sewing market, needle companies have been busy designing new types of needles to solve sewing problems associated with this new technology. Traditional sewers will relate this information to their sewing machines, but "sergeons" also can take advantage of this useful information and adapt it to their serger sewing and embellishment. The only limitation to using any needle type in an overlock machine is in relation to its size, as sergers are designed to use only sizes #70, #80, and #90 needles.

Sew, what's the point of it all?

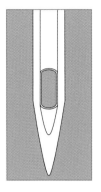

We now have a variety of needle types to meet our specific needs. By understanding the design of the various specialty needle types, the sewer will understand more completely how to choose the best type of needle for constructing or embellishing a garment. Gone are the days of simply deciding whether to use a sharp or ballpoint needle!

Microfibers and other densely woven fabrics, such as denims, silks, and sand-washed rayons, benefit from using a needle which has a thinner and sharper point. Some of these fabrics, though fine and silky in appearance, are manufactured with very fine and tightly woven fibers which are difficult to penetrate when sewing without skipping stitches. Needles labeled "microfiber" or Microtex-sharp range in sizes #60 through #100.

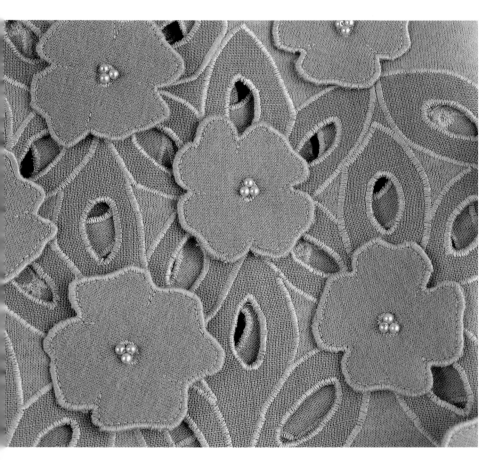

It also should be noted that when sewing with microfibers, the needle points need to be absolutely free of burrs or sharp edges. Points that show the slightest unevenness will damage the fabric to a greater extent than a needle which is too thick or has an improper point. Needle points, therefore, require checking more regularly.

This new microfiber needle design also is terrific for French hand sewing by machine, a technique which frequently uses delicate fabrics and laces. A jeans needle, which is similar in design to a microfiber needle, can be used as a substitute.

Embroidery needles have been developed to accommodate metallic and other novelty threads which are increasing in popularity. Similar to a topstitch needle, the embroidery needle has a larger eye than a standard Universal sewing needle and the groove on the front profile is large in size providing better thread protection and handling. This needle design also has a new scarf that allows the needle to form a better loop during stitch formation, also reducing the risk of skipped stitches and shredded threads. The point has been designed to eliminate damaging the fabric and thread. Since the point is slightly rounded, it can be used either on knit or woven fabrics. Its slightly larger eye also is suitable for combining two or three threads and is available in sizes #70 - #90. A topstitch needle which is extra sharp and a similar design with a large groove and an extra-large eye, is a viable substitute for embroidery needles.

Since metallic threads are more delicate and have a tendency to shred, fray, and break easily, a metallic needle has been created with a rounded point, a deeper groove down the

front, and a much larger eye that is coated with a product similar to Teflon.

Quilters, too, have found creative ways in constructing and embellishing quilts and quilt-related articles. The quilting needle, which has a special taper design to the point, is used to prevent damage to the great variety of materials used in quilting and provides ease in sewing transverse seams.

Twin or double needles are produced in a variety of sizes with varying spaces between the needles. The spacing and needle size are typically noted on the package or container, such as 1.6/80 indicates a 1.6mm space between the needles and #80 is the needle size. Double needles are also available in 2.0, 2.5, 3.0, 4.0, 6.0, and 8.0mm sizes. The last two sizes are restricted to sewing machines that have a stitch width beyond 5.0mm and up to 9mm.

Single-wing needles have a flattened and tapered section on the needle shaft which enables the needle to make an enlarged entry hole into the fabric. It perforates the fabric intentionally to decoratively sew on fine fabrics such as cottons, linens and silks. Double-wing needles are similar to a twin needle except that one of the needles is a standard needle and the other is shaped like a single-wing needle.

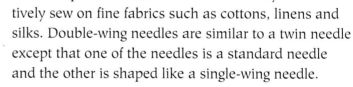

Threads

Thread plays an important and critical role in appliqué or any other machine art. Decorative machine threads are made in a wide variety of fibers and textures. They range from l00% cotton in #30, #50, and #60 weights; rayon in #30 and #40 weights; silk; monofilament; wool; wool with an acrylic mixture; and several metallic- and tinsel-type threads. Reserve your polyester thread for its functional role in constructing a garment.

Acrylic thread resembles rayon very closely with its high sheen and is considered slightly stronger by some embroiderers. It is used in some cutwork when using a chemical to dissolve natural fiber fabric. The thread is not affected by the chemical treatment.

Since most fine embroidery threads are not made with the high twist required of ordinary sewing threads, they are more fragile and are not recommended for sewing seams. Remember to use one of the

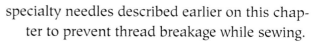

specialty needles described earlier on this chapter to prevent thread breakage while sewing. Combine two or three fine rayon or cotton threads in the same needle for highlighting textures. An extra thread stand or thread palette aids in the proper feeding of the multiple threads through the thread guides and tension on the machine.

The thread used for the bobbin is usually of a finer weight, such as #60 cotton, and does not necessarily have to match the needle thread. If the back of the work is visible as in cutwork, use the same thread in the bobbin as in the needle. Heavier threads which can not be placed through the eye of a needle are used on the bobbin. An extra bobbin case with tension slightly loosened will accommodate heavier thicknesses of threads. Adjust the tension screw slowly until the desired tension is evident. Dependable heavier threads and yarns include six-strand embroidery floss, which is also available in rayon and silk versions. Additional threads include heavier metallics, heavier single-strand twisted and untwisted rayons, topstitching threads, ribbon floss, and a vari-

ety of knitting and crochet yarns or yarns unraveled from your fabric. Any thread or yarn can be used as long as it passes through the bobbin tension area smoothly. Occasionally, it may be necessary to remove the tension screw entirely, but those situations are rare.

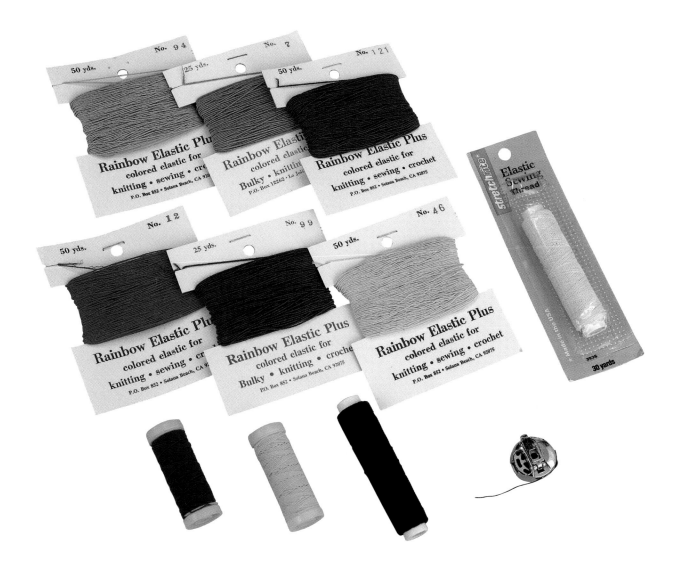

Elastic thread, though not used to edge motifs, is exciting and interesting to use in creating the fabric for the motif. Available in lightweight and medium-weight versions, it comes in a good selection of colors so that either the right side or wrong side of the motif can be used once it is stitched. Treat the elastic thread like any other thicker thread when winding the bobbin on the machine.

Since heavier thread in the bobbin requires more help to hold it against the fabric, needle tensions should be tightened. Start slowly and increase the tension to maximum. The right combination of bobbin and needle tension will give you the results desired. If the needle thread shows through to the right side, try using monofilament thread in the needle for invisible coverage.

Stabilizers and Underlinings

Underlinings and stabilizers are important for supporting a wide variety of fabrics and threads during and after the process of decorative sewing and/ or serging. The following under-linings and stabilizers are categorized according to their uniqueness and relavance to fabric and threads.

Underlinings

Underlinings are the permanently placed, hidden component that provides shape and support to embellished fabric. A good stable backing material not only will prolong the life of the garment but also will enhance its appearance.

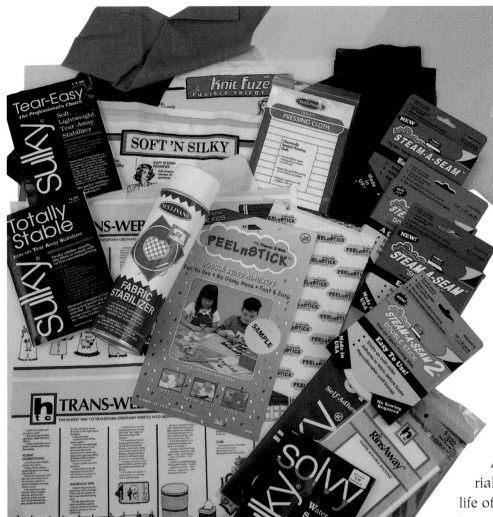

When selecting underlining material, consider the weight of the garment fabric and the amount of softness or crispness desired. Weight is an important factor, as the backing should be lighter than the garment fabric. If too light, it will not provide the desired stability. In contrast, if it is too heavy, it will weigh down your garment and distort the shape and stitching.

The following interfacings are used as underlinings for the purposes mentioned above:

Fusible knits, which are 100% nylon, are available in light to medium weights and are perhaps the most commonly used interfacing.

A fusible tricot knit is suitable for most woven and knit fabrics as it has lengthwise stability and crosswise stretch for soft shaping, underlining and reinforcement.

For use on medium-weight, silk-like fabrics, synthetic suedes, knits, and wovens, choose a 100% polyester fusible knit that consists of a warp insertion with all bias stretch. It is also ideal for sand-washed silks, microfibers, and other heat sensitive fabrics.

For delicate fabrics, especially those which cannot take a high-heat setting or on fabrics on which the fusible underlining will show after fusing, choose a 100% rayon underlining fused at a silk setting. A light, temporary bond will be created and the underlining will eventually separate from the garment fabric. This type of underlining is marvelous in providing extra support when handling particularly slinky or slippery varieties of fabrics.

Stabilizers

TEAR-AWAY AND WATER-SOLUBLE STABILIZERS

Tear-away stabilizers have been available for several years and come in a variety of weights. They should be strong enough to support the fabric, stitches and embellished design and still have the capacity to tear easily in both horizontal and vertical directions without putting stress on either the garment or the decorative stitches. It is sometimes preferable to use two or three layers of tear-away for extra support rather than use the extra thick variety, as the lighter version does not leave as much of the tear-away residue within the stitches.

Another variety of tear-away is an evenly perforated material suitable for stabilizing most fabrics. It has a slip-resistant backing which allows greater stability while stitching and then tears away cleanly in all directions.

A lightweight tear-away backing which washes away when laundered may be desired when it is necessary to completely remove the stabilizer. Some fibers may still remain near the stitched areas but will eventually dissolve in subsequent launderings.

A type of stabilizer that has a coating on one side and is used against the wrong side of the fabric is great when working on knits or other stretchy-type fabrics. It is pressed with a warm iron, which temporarily adheres it to the fabric giving additional support. On an extensive project, it may be necessary to do additional pressing before the stitching is completed.

Water-soluable stabilizers can be used under and/or over the fabric and is particularly useful on napped or pile fabrics, such as towels, knits, velveteens, or corduroy, to prevent stitches from becoming "lost" in the fabric. When the project is completed, gently tear away any excess stabilizer, then spray lightly with water or steam to dissolve the remaining film. Be sure to allow enough time for dissolving the stabilizer - up to 45 to 60 seconds. For a firmer backing, press two or three layers together using a good press cloth or preferably a Teflon™ press sheet. In humid climates, remember to store this stabilizer in an air-tight plastic bag.

Another variety working on a similar concept is a woven stabilizer which requires nearly boiling water for removal.

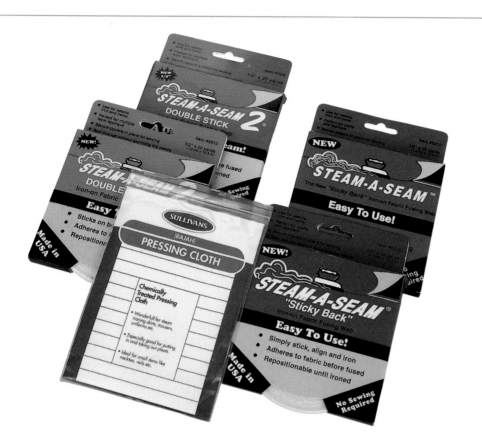

HOT TAPE

A rather unique, heat-resistant tape, this revolutionary new adhesive holds under the hottest iron and, when removed leaves no residue on either the fabric or the iron. It eliminates pins and pinholes and is reusable. Printed like a 5/8" tape measure, it is available on three-yard rolls with dispenser, backed refill rolls and handy tape tabs. It will take five minutes of continuous heat and is ideal for transfers, quilting, sewing appliqué, serging, and other crafts. You do not sew through this tape but use it for positioning.

LIQUID STABILIZERS

Liquid stabilizers are either dipped or painted onto the fabric. These products also keep fabric edges from fraying while sewing or serging. Some varieties are very similar to spray starch. Depending upon the fabric and embellishment techniques used, more than one coating may be necessary. Water-soluable stabilizers also can be be liquified by dissolving approximately 1 yard of stabilizer in 1 cup of water. This method offers another alternative to traditional liquid stabilizers.

HEAT-SENSITIVE
BRUSH-OFF STABILIZERS:

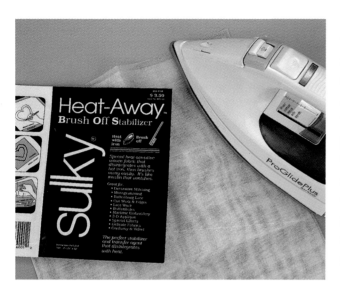

This type of stabilizer is the answer for projects where wetting or tearing would cause distortion to stitches or damage to the fabrics. Place the heat-sensitive stabilizer under or over the fabric or design area to be stitched, and pin or baste in place. Once the stitching is completed, the stabilizer will disintegrate by placing a dry hot iron (cotton or linen setting) on it until it turns brown (approximately 10 - 15 seconds). Gently brush away the brown "crumbs" with a soft bristle brush, such as a toothbrush. For more delicate fabrics try a lower heat setting for a slightly longer time and protect them with a press cloth between the iron and stabilizer.

PAPER-BACKED FUSIBLES

This type of stabilizer is mainly associated with appliqué. It is a polyamide web on release paper. Trace the motifs on the paper side. Preheat an iron to a light to medium setting, but do not overheat as it may cause an insufficient bond. Place the fusible side against the wrong side of the fabric and press on the paper side for 1 to 4 seconds. Carefully cut out the motifs and peel the paper backing from the fabric. Place the fusible side of the motif against the right side of the base fabric and press for 3 to 5 seconds to adhere. Dimensional motifs are created by fusing two layers of fabric together with paper-backed stabilizer and then edging with decorative threads by sewing machine or serger.

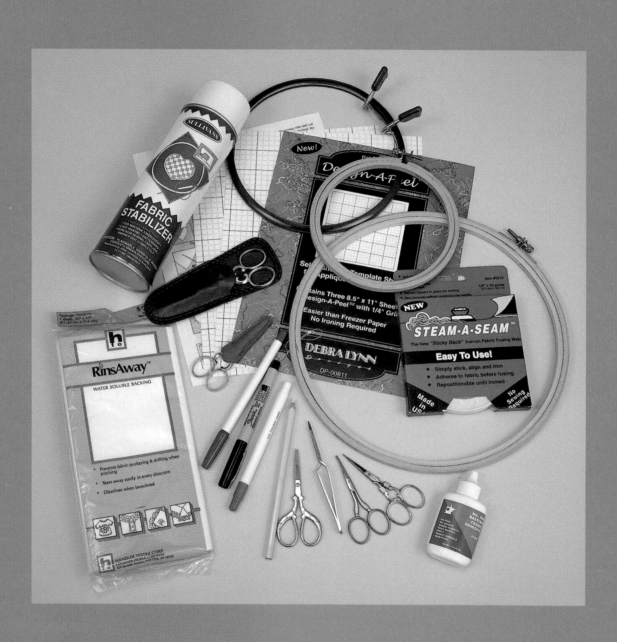

THE BASIC TOOLS

Notions

Marking Pens

An assortment of fabric marking pens, transfer pens and tailor's chalk for use on a variety of fabrics will greatly reduce preparation and marking time. Fine-to medium-point black permanent markers are handy for indelibly outlining and designing templates along with identifying personal equipment.

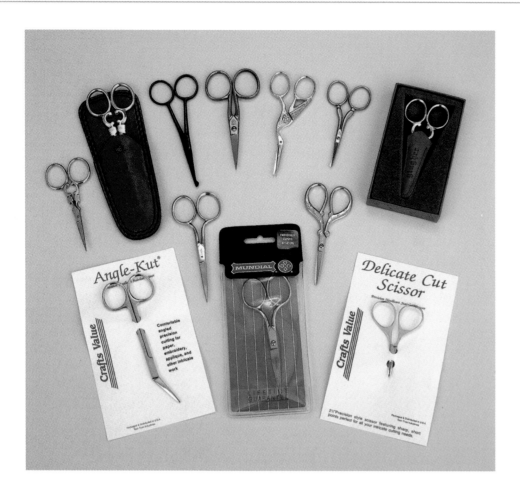

Cutting Equipment

Sharp shears and scissors in a variety of sizes will eliminate snagged edges. If you use both synthetic and natural-fiber fabrics, labeling your scissors for each purpose will keep your scissors sharp for a longer period of time. For instance, purchase two of the same type of cutting scissors and label one: Synthetic Fabrics and the other Natural Fabrics.

Small and large appliqué scissors, which consist of one pelican-shaped blade, will prevent you from cutting into the fabric base. Small curved and straight embroidery scissors and snipers are additional types for fine cutwork and for those hard to reach areas. Identify a small pair of scissors for cutting paper, vinyl, and plastic templates.

To simplify and expedite time involved in cutting long and straight edges, a rotary cutter and cutting mat are invaluable tools.

Hoops

A spring-loaded plastic hoop may be used for short-term use, though it cannot be adjusted for firmness. A machine-embroidery wooden hoop with cut-out areas for easier handling under the presser foot is preferable and will keep the fabric from slipping. It is also desirable for more elaborate projects. By wrapping the inner hoop with bias tape or torn bias strips of fabric, tautness can be further guaranteed. It would be helpful to have several sizes of hoops in each style.

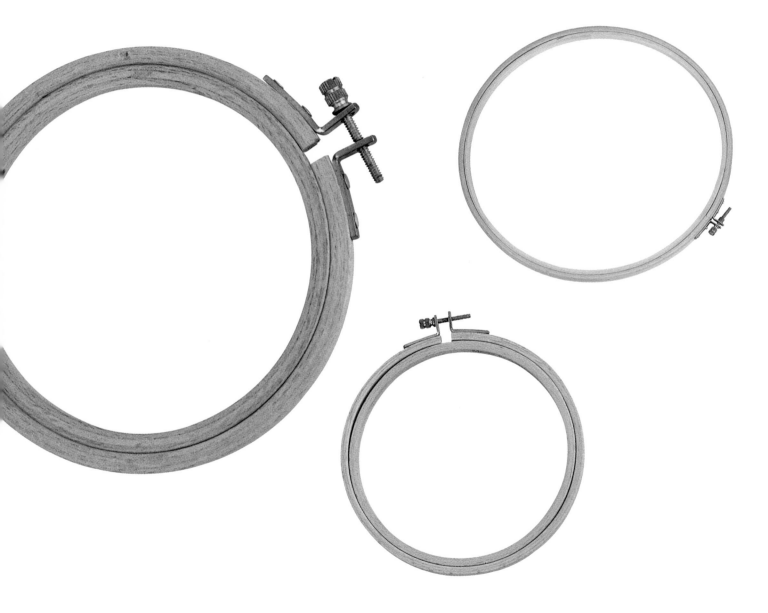

Additional sewing aids, such as a light box for tracing; seam sealant; needle threaders; tweezers; tracing vellum for pattern-making; clear, frosted, and grided plastic of vinyl template-making material; and even a soft bristled toothbrush for raising naps on napped and piled fabrics, are all helpful additions to the sewing room.

Pressing Matters

A good steam iron that holds its heat on the fabric's ideal setting along with a sturdy ironing board is essential. Plan on having two ironing board covers.

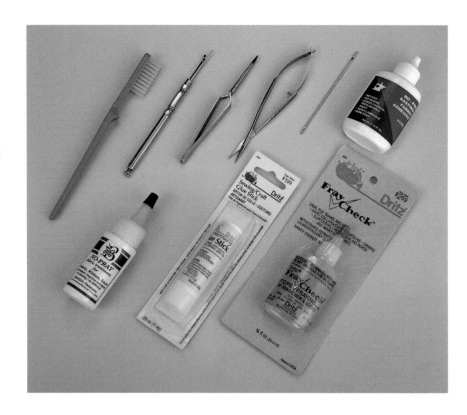

Use one for your everyday ironing activity and one for embellishment pressing. Light- and heavyweight press cloths will protect heat sensitive and fragile fabrics. A Teflon™ press sheet will protect napped fabrics and metallic threads. An ironing press for fusing large pieces of fabric speeds the pressing process as will a commercial steam ironing system and a handheld steamer.

For some decorative applications, using heavy spray starch may be necessary; spray sizing may be useful for final light pressing to protect decorative threads from abrasion.

SEWING MACHINE PREPARATION

Satin-Stitch Guidelines

The traditional method of applying appliqués to the base fabric is with a satin stitch. It is the mark of quality work to achieve a beautiful, smooth stitch appropriate in size and weight to the motif.

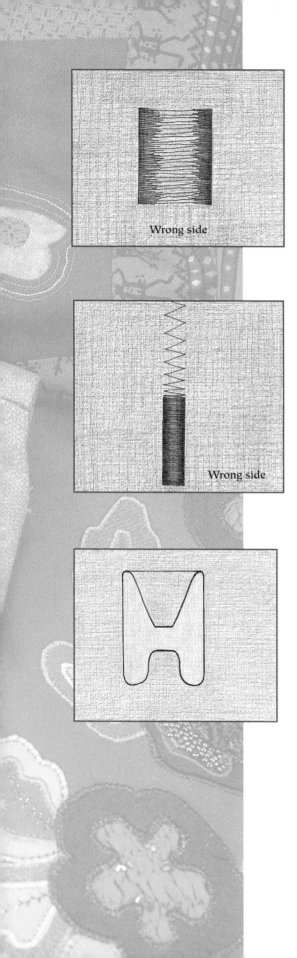

Thread Tension

There are a couple of simple tension adjustments which are necessary for a basic and smooth satin stitch. Since in most appliqué and embroidery projects the weights of threads in the needle and bobbin case are different, you will use a loose top thread tension. This will draw the needle thread to the underside completely, give a smoother appearance along the edges, and eliminate the need to change bobbin threads every time you change the top thread.

Stitch Length

The stitch length should be set so that the threads stitched into the fabric are laying as close together as possible, side by side, similar to a satin ribbon. Minor fine tuning adjustments will be necessary with varying weights of threads and dyes.

Stitch Width

The stitch width should be chosen according to the size of your motif design. Try using the most narrow width that you think you can get away with to ensure motif security and appearance. When sewing on the appliqué motif, the major part of your satin stitch should fall on the motif, not on the background fabric. Stitch so that the outside swing of the needle falls just off the edge of the fabric.

Remember to use your embroidery foot for best results. The underside of the foot is cut away to allow smooth feeding of the stain stitch.

Securing the Stitches

The satin stitch can be secured easily if you have a securing function on your sewing machine. Otherwise, you can either lower the feed dogs and stitch in place for three or four single straight stitches, or set the stitch length on 0 with the feed dogs up.

Curves, Corners, and Points

Curves

OUTSIDE CURVE: STITCH on the curve of the motif design until the line of stitching starts to move away from the curve. With the needle down **in the fabric base**, lift the presser foot and reposition the fabric under the presser foot slightly so that the stitches will overlap as you continue to complete the curve. Gentle curves will take less repositioning than tight small curves.

INSIDE CURVE: This process is handled similar to the outside curve with the following exception - stop with the needle down **in the appliqué motif** and continue to overlap stitches slightly while stitching the inside curve, as above.

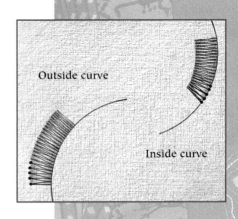

SCALLOP DESIGNS: Stitch past the point which would be equal to the width of your zigzag stitch. Pivot with the needle on the left side, raise the presser foot, and with the raw edge once again lined up on the inside of the presser foot, continue stitching.

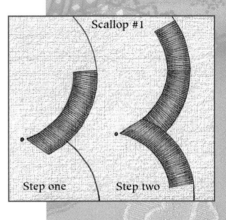

OR

With your hand on the stitch-width dial, slowly decrease the width to 0 while stitching past the point which would be equal to the width of your zigzag stitch. Lower the needle, pivot, and slowly increase the width as you approach the area which is to be sewn at your original width setting.

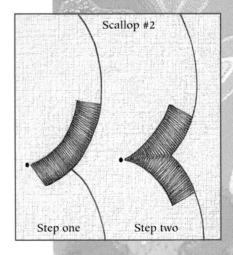

Corners

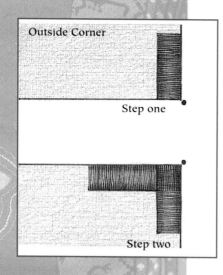

OUTSIDE CORNER: Stitch to the edge of the corner, stopping with the needle down on the outside corner of the motif. Raise the presser foot and pivot so that the edge to be stitched is parallel with the presser foot. Lower the presser foot and continue stitching, overlapping stitches at the corner.

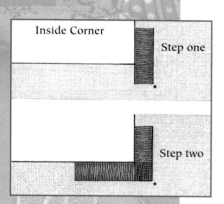

INSIDE CORNER: Stitch to the corner continuing to stitch into the appliqué motif the distance if your stitch width. Raise the presser foot and pivot so that the edge to be stitched is parallel with the presser foot. Lower the presser foot and continue stitching.

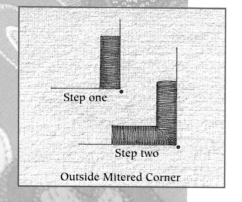

OUTSIDE MITERED CORNER: Stitch all the way to the corner. Pivot and turn the corner with the needle in the fabric. With the stitch width set at 0, gradually increase the width while stitching, until you have reached the original width.

OR

Stitch to the corner, pivot and then engage a triangular decorative stitch. Stop stitching in the middle of the design. Note: Some machines have a function that will automatically stop halfway into the stitch. Complete stitching the edge with the original satin-stitch width.

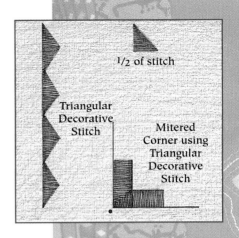

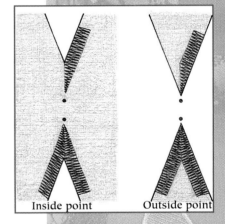

Points

OUTSIDE AND INSIDE POINTS: To stitch points so they look nice and clean, gradually reduce the width of the stitches as you approach the point. When you have reached the end of the point, lower the needle, pivot, and continue to stitch the other side by gradually increasing the stitch width until you are back to the original width.

OR

When you are two or three stitches from the point, stop and "walk" the needle around the point until you are in a position to stitch on a continual path again. "Walking" the needle requires you to stitch one stitch at a time, lowering the needle each time and turning until the entire point is covered and looks smooth.

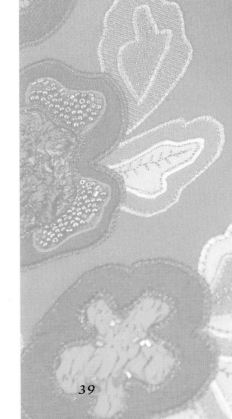

Presser Feet

It is important to use a special presser foot that has been designed for satin stitching when appliquéing.

BASIC EMBROIDERY/APPLIQUÉ FOOT: This foot has a wide groove under the foot and may have a hole in front of the foot which can be used for couching fine cords.

OPEN EMBROIDERY FOOT: Similar to the basic embroidery/ appliqué foot with a wide groove underneath, it has the bar between the toes in front removed for greater visibility.

TEFLON™ OPEN EMBROIDERY FOOT: This foot has a Teflon™ coating on the sole for use on fabrics that hinder presser foot movement, such as faux and natural leathers; vinyl; and coated, glossy, or slippery fabrics.

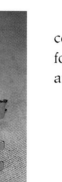

The following feet are useful when using free-motion techniques:

DARNING FOOT, FREEHAND EMBROIDERY FOOT (similar to a darning foot but cut away in front), and LARGE DARNING FOOT (accommodates wide zigzag stitch): When these feet are used with the feed dogs lowered, the spring action allows these feet to stay closer to the fabric while the needle progresses up and out of the fabric. This opposite needle and foot movement prevents the fabric from flagging or moving up and down.

ROLLER FOOT: This presser foot has two sets of rollers underneath, which aid in stitching over fabrics that tend to hinder normal presser-foot movement.

GATHERING FOOT: This foot will not only gather but will encourage stubborn fabric to scrunch while using elastic thread in the bobbin.

TAILOR TACK FOOT: Used for added embellishments, the center metal configuration of the foot enables the satin stitch to form raised loops for creating fringe.

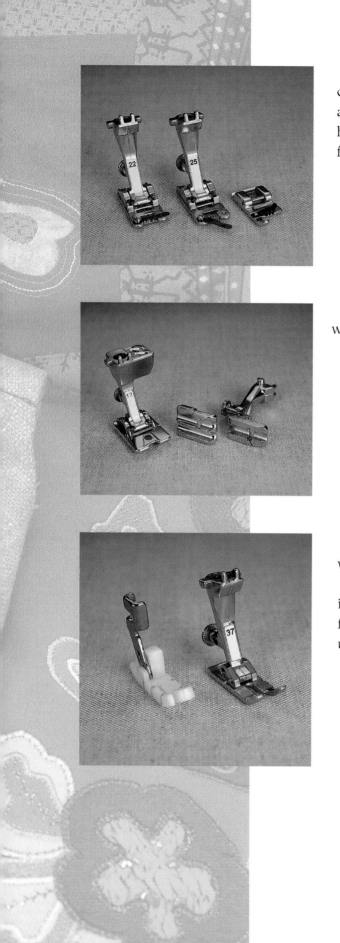

COUCHING FEET: There are a variety of presser feet used for couching single or multiple strands of threads, strung beads and sequins, and assorted sizes of yarns and ribbons. Each has its own special design characteristics which prevent cords from wandering.

PIPING FOOT: This foot has a large tunnel on the bottom, which is perfect for holding beads, firm trims and piping.

BRAIDING FOOT: This foot keeps very narrow braids in place while stitching.

PATCHWORK OR ¼" FOOT: This presser foot is handy when incorporating appliqué techniques with quilting or when perfect ¼" rows of straight stitching are needed. It is particularly useful with fine elastic thread.

EYELET ATTACHMENT: This device makes a variety of eyelet sizes and will add that third dimension to appliqué motifs. Some machines have one or two basic eyelet stitches built in, which also work well on some designs.

EXTRA BOBBIN CASE: An extra bobbin case comes in handy for handling thicker threads, yarns, ribbons, and elastic thread. The tension screw on the bobbin case requires loosening in accordance with the thickness of the threads.

APPLIQUÉ-TIONS

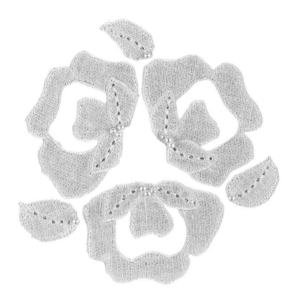

Basic Appliqué Instructions

There are some preliminary motif and fabric preparations which contribute to the success of an appliqué project. By following these basic principles, the process of assembling and building most appliqué designs will go more smoothly and quickly. The simple steps of tracing, pressing, cutting, and fusing make the stitching easier and enhance the durability of the garment or project.

Materials and Supplies:

❖ Appliqué fabric of choice
❖ Paper-backed fusible web
❖ Fabric marking pen or fine-point permanent marking pen
❖ Clear vinyl for templates
❖ Assorted base fabric scissors
❖ Paper-cutting scissors
❖ Iron
❖ Tear-away stabilizer
❖ Cotton, rayon, or metallic embroidery thread

Tracing Motif Designs

Method A

1. Trace the appliqué motif onto the paper side of the fusible web with either a fabric marking pen or a fine-point permanent marking pen. The design will be mirror-imaged on the fusible webbing after tracing.

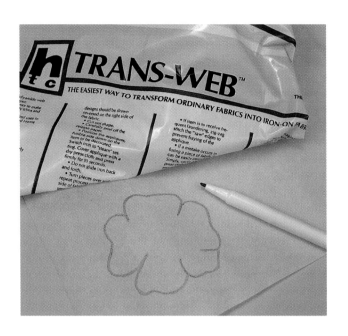

> **SEWING TIP**
>
> Refrain from using a pencil or ballpoint pen for tracing appliqués onto the paper-backed fusible web as it will rub off on the fabric.

2. Press the fusible side of the traced motif onto the wrong side of the appliqué fabric. Cut out the motif along the design lines.

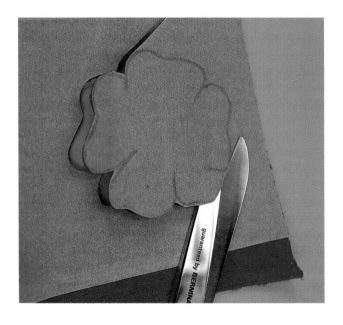

Stitching Motif Designs

3. Remove the paper backing from each motif. Following your overall design, position the motif pieces on the background fabric layering appropriately. Fuse each piece securely in place.

4. Pin or baste a piece of tear-away stabilizer — cut 2" - 3" larger than the design area — to the wrong side of the background fabric. The tear-away stabilizer will be next to the feed dogs when stitching.
5. Stitch each appliqué piece in place using your stitch of choice. Adjust the stitch width to the overall size of the appliqué design. Refer to the Satin-Stitch Guidelines on page 37.

Method B

Vinyl templates are an asset in the design process. They are transparent and helpful when attempting to choose certain colors in the motif fabrics. They will last a long time, can be used repeatedly, and allow you to preserve the integrity of your design while you are working on it.

SEWING TIP

Prepare more vinyl templates than you think you will need. They come in handy with unexpected design combinations. Use the templates to create the overall design placement directly on the garment or project.

1. Create templates by drawing the design motifs directly onto the clear vinyl with a permanent marking pen. Cut out the individual templates with paper-cutting scissors.

2. Use the vinyl templates to trace the motifs onto the paper-backed fusible web as described in step 1 of Method A. *Note:* When working with an unusual fabric design or if a particular color within the fabric is desired, fuse a large piece of the appliqué fabric to the paper-backed fusible web first. Then position the clear vinyl template on the right side of the fabric where you want it and trace around it to obtain the best design.

3. Continue your appliquéing process following steps 2 through 5 in Method A.

Finishing the Motifs

When all the stitching has been completed, remove any tear-away stabilizer and press the completed project with the appropriate press cloth.

SEWING TIP

Remember to select the correct stabilizers, interfacings, underlinings, and special press cloths that work best on more fragile and sensitive fabrics and threads.

THE PROJECTS

A Hole-in-One Appliqué

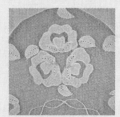

Corded Appliqué

Cutwork Appliqué

Elastications

Reverse or Non-Traditional Mola Appliqué

Sheer Elegance Appliqué

Tone-on-Tone Appliqué

Upside-Down Appliqué

Wool Appliqué

HOLE-IN-ONE APPLIQUÉ

Sports enthusiasts will typically play their games "come rain or come shine." Ready-to-wear sports departments and specialty sports stores sell garments made from new fabrics that either repel or resist light drizzles enabling the person to continue his or her game. Having made my husband, Hank, several of these outfits in the past, I designed the following project just for him.

An avid golfer, Hank will go to great lengths to play golf. During a period of semiretirement, he accompanied me on several trips around this country and Australia while I indulged in teaching tours and he explored different golf courses. We have met many wonderful people throughout our travels, and it is not unusual to receive an inquiry to teach classes from a previously visited store followed by the additional comment, "Will Hank be coming too? We found another golf course for Hank."

Densely woven and treated fabrics like those used in rainwear require special considerations. The needles should be sharp, a Microtex or Jeans needle, to eliminate skipped stitches. Since these fabrics take very little heat, pressing also is an important issue to prevent melting or distortion from taking place. A Teflon™ press sheet or an appropriate substitute is necessary to have on hand.

When sewing on this type of rainwear fabric, traditional satin-stitch appliqué techniques aren't appropriate since tunneling or puckering results from too much thread on such a densely woven fabric. Most of the appliqué motifs used on these pieces are from non-woven fabrics.

Non-woven fabric motifs are either straight stitched (edgestitched) onto the base fabric, zigzagged with a very narrow stitch width, or appliquéd with a blanket stitch and monofilament thread. If a woven fabric is used, such as the grass on the "9th Hole", the motif must be first satin stitched onto the non-woven before then edge-stitched to the rainwear fabric.

Materials and Supplies:

❖ Rainwear fabric of choice; yardage as required on pattern

❖ 100% cotton flannel for shirt and jacket sections

❖ 5 - 7¼ yard of 100% cotton and non-woven fabrics (Ultrasuede™ or Ultraleather™) for motifs

❖ Monofilament thread

❖ Teflon ™ open embroidery foot

❖ Rayon embroidery thread in matching colors

❖ 2 yards of batiste or muslin for underlining

Appliqué Instructions:

1. Cut the pattern pieces from the rainwear fabric taking into consideration the following: The jacket fronts were replaced with 100% cotton flannel, cut into four pieces from two different-size check designs. By using the cotton flannel as the base, more freedom and versatility was allowed in the appliqué treatment used. To prevent any moisture from coming through, the rainwear fabric was used as the lining for the fronts. The jacket back lining is the cotton flannel appliquéd with golf clubs using the Basic Appliqué technique. After the motifs are appliquéd onto the four blocks of checked fabric, they are placed onto an underlining fabric, such as a lightweight batiste or muslin. The edges are butted together and a 2"-wide strip of rainwear fabric is topstitched over the seams to tie all the pieces together.

2. Following the Basic Appliqué Instructions, steps 1 through 4, cut the **golf shoe** motifs from white and blue Ultrasuede™ and Ultraleather™ fabric. Edgestitch the heel and sole with blue thread.

3. Edgestitch the second shoe with two lines of stitching emphasizing the heel area.

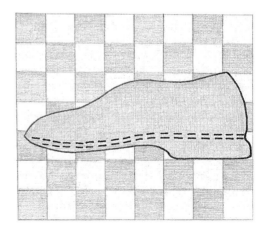

4. Edge- or satin-stitch the blue side piece in place. For the flap motif, allow approximately ¾" in length for the fringe. Stitch in place and cut the fringe.

5. Using silver metallic thread, create metal studs on the sole by lowering your feed dogs and zigzag (stitch length: 0 and stitch width: 2mm) in place three or four times.

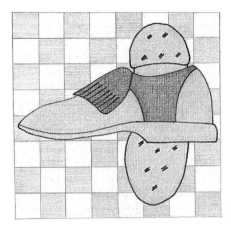

6. To create the **golfer** in the lower panel, prepare the motifs according to the Basic Appliqué Instructions, steps 1 through 4. Cut the hands, face, legs, and cap from Ultrasuede™; the top and knickers from two coordinating cotton fabrics.

7. Satin-stitch the golf club beginning with a 2mm stitch width tapering to a 5mm.

8. To attach the hands, legs, face and cap with monofilament thread, zigzag (stitch length and stitch width: 1mm) the pieces in place.

9. Satin-stitch (stitch length: satin stitch and stitch width: 1.5mm) the pants and shirt with a coordinating thread color.

10. For the **golf bag** in the upper panel, prepare the motifs according to the Basic Appliqué Instructions. Straight-stitch the silver and gold faux-leather golf clubs in place.

11. Satin-stitch (stitch length: satin stitch and stitch width: 2mm) the golf bag in place with a coordinating thread color.

12. Prepare the motifs for the **golf tee** in the lower panel according to the Basic Appliqué Instructions. Satin-stitch (stitch length: satin stitch and stitch width: 2mm) the golf ball first, then layer the tee.

13. Prepare the motifs for the **"9th Hole"** on the back of the jacket according to the Basic Appliqué Instructions, steps 1 through 4. Satin-stitch the green cotton print tee onto the green Ultrasuede™ fabric.

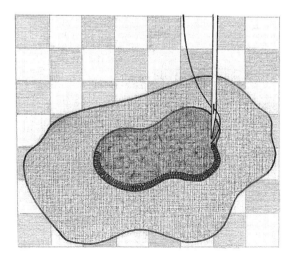

14. Satin-stitch the golf ball tapering the stitch while sewing.
15. To create the black hole, zigzag (stitch length and width: 1mm) a small piece of Ultrasuede™ using monofilament thread.
16. Edgestitch the golf green onto the jacket back.
17. With monofilament thread, zigzag (stitch length and width: 1mm) the flag pole and flag in place. As an optional decorative touch, embroider the number 9 on the tee flag.

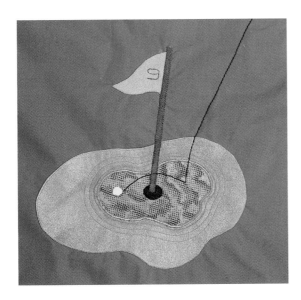

18. Following the pattern given, straight-stitch lines from the shoulder area to the "missed" tee area with topstitching thread. Two rayon threads placed through the same needle eye also work well.

19. For the jacket lining, arrange the **clubs** in a crisscross fashion and edgestitch the club handles in place.

20. Satin-stitch (stitch length: stain stitch and stitch width: 2mm) a variety of cotton prints for the club heads. Emphasize club head shapes with additional satin-stitch lines as shown.

❖ Accessories can be added to this outfit for the avid golfer in your life!

❖ Black Hat: Using decorative stitches, monogram his initials on the hat band front before assembling.

❖ Rust Supplex™ Cap: Embroider or appliqué a tiny teeing green on the front.

❖ Cotton flannel shirt: Decorate the right shirt front, collar, and cuffs with preset computer designs of golfers. Monogram the shirt pocket with a preset golf emblem.

Hank's tip: Get your sewing tips from a golf pro!

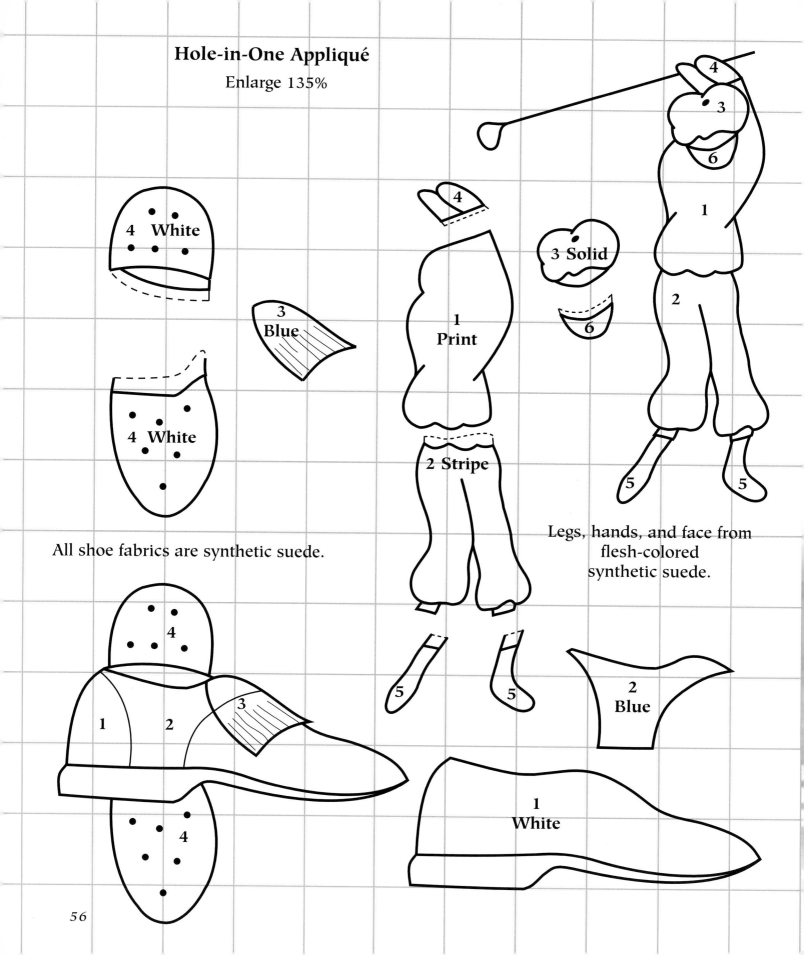

Hole-in-One Appliqué
Enlarge 135%

4 White

3 Blue

4 White

All shoe fabrics are synthetic suede.

4

1 Print

2 Stripe

3 Solid

6

Legs, hands, and face from flesh-colored synthetic suede.

4

3

6

1

2

5

5

5

5

1

2

3

4

4

2 Blue

1 White

56

Hole-in-One Appliqué

Enlarge 135%

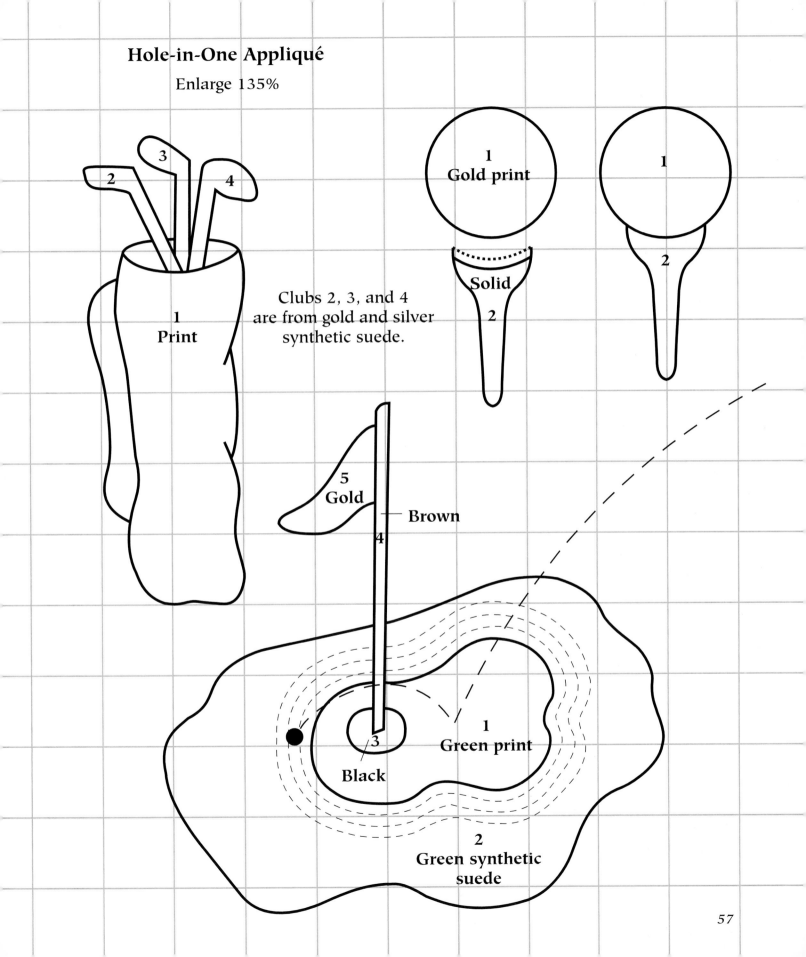

3

2

4

1
Print

1
Gold print

Solid

2

1

2

Clubs 2, 3, and 4
are from gold and silver
synthetic suede.

5
Gold

Brown

4

3

Black

1
Green print

2
Green synthetic
suede

57

Hole-in-One Appliqué

Enlarge 135%

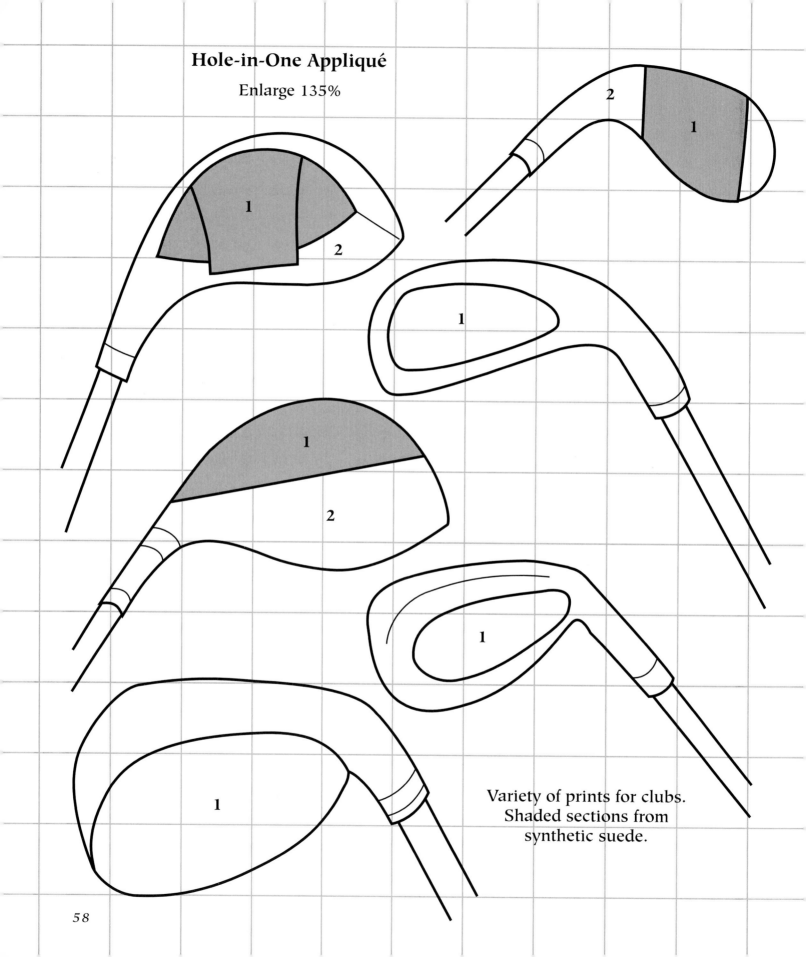

Variety of prints for clubs.
Shaded sections from
synthetic suede.

CORDED APPLIQUÉ

Corded appliqué simply means to attach a cord to the raw edge of the motif design with an open zigzag stitch prior to satin stitching. The diameter of the cord depends upon the weight of the garment and the motif fabrics. It's important to note that cord that is too heavy will look "overweight" or overpower the entire garment or project.

Cords add strength and stability to outline designs on necklines and fabrics such as knits, sheers, laces, and metallics. Couched with an open zigzag stitch only, the cord also may be used to enhance the inner parts of designs, such as flower centers and veins on leaves. There are many examples of cords that can be used in this type of appliqué: topstitching threads, such as Cordonnet; crochet cottons; yarn; fishing line; or kite string. Pearl cotton is particularly easy to work with as it's available in a variety of weights and sizes.

Materials and Supplies:

- ❖ Fabric yardage as required on pattern plus ½ yard
- ❖ Fine, fusible tricot (Sew Sheer™) for reinforcing seam edges, as necessary
- ❖ Strips of nylon tricot (Seams Great™) for stabilizing shoulder and sleeve cap seams, as necessary
- ❖ #60 cotton embroidery or bobbinfil
- ❖ #30 or #40 cotton or rayon embroidery threads in two very close shades (one will be used to define leaf veins only)
- ❖ Water-soluble or burn-away stabilzer

Appliqué Instructions:

1. Follow the Basic Appliqué Instructions, steps 1 through 3, to prepare the motif designs. Fuse the cut appliqué motifs in place on the background fabric.
2. Thread your sewing machine and bobbin with the appropriate threads and machine baste a stabilizer 1½" to 2" from the edge of the motifs around the entire design.

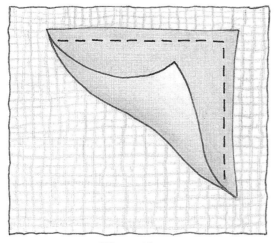

Wrong side

3. Select a zigzag (stitch length: 1mm and stitch width: 1½mm) and couch the cord around all the designated areas including the veins of the leaves. Begin couching the cord at an inconspicuous spot on the motif, providing a smooth starting and stopping point. Fine-tune the zigzag setting while stitching so the stitch width barely covers the cord. Use a securing stitch on your machine to start and end your stitching.

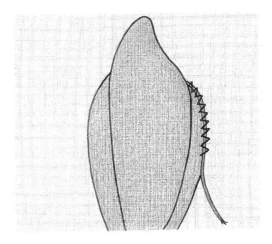

SEWING TIP

Use a stitch length and width of 0 to lock your stitches in place at the beginning and end of your satin stitch.

4. Continue to outline all of the motif edges following the "bottoms up" format. Begin stitching on the bottom layer and work up. Though the flower and leaf designs are quite similar, try to vary the definition of the foreground petals, leaves, and leaf veins. This will add to the natural look and overall interest of the design.

SEWING TIP

To keep the cord from wandering on outer and inner pivot points, lower the needle in the left position on outer points and in the right position on inner pivot points before turning. This is contrary to the regular satin stitching technique.

5. Satin stitch over the cord on all the edges of the flowers, stems, and leaves.

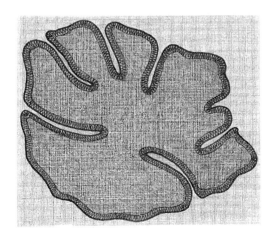

6. Use a triple straight stitch or multi-motion straight stitch as indicated on the pattern to create the stamen. Add a decorative stitch,

such as a small satin stitch oval, at the ends. Shorten the stitch length and width according to the flower's size or, if possible, use the double-needle function and balance button on your machine to reduce the size of the decorative stitch.

7. Some of the "forward" flower petals may be shaded by using a random zigzag stitch width or a built-in decorative stitch found on some computerized sewing machines. Or stitch a random zigzag stitch along the inner edges. Add beads to the ends of the decorative stitches for further enhancement.

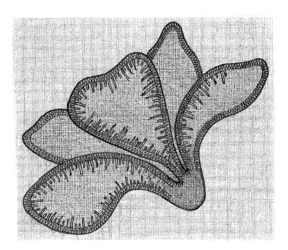

8. To create the dimensional centers, use a water-soluble or burn-away stabilizer and follow the instructions in "Cutwork Applique", steps 12 and 13. Remove the stabilizer according to the manufacturer's directions. Cord and satin stitch the stand-away edges.

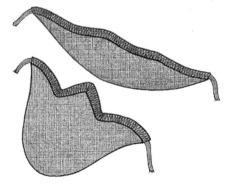

9. Attach the remaining sections of the flower and bud motifs with a satin stitch.

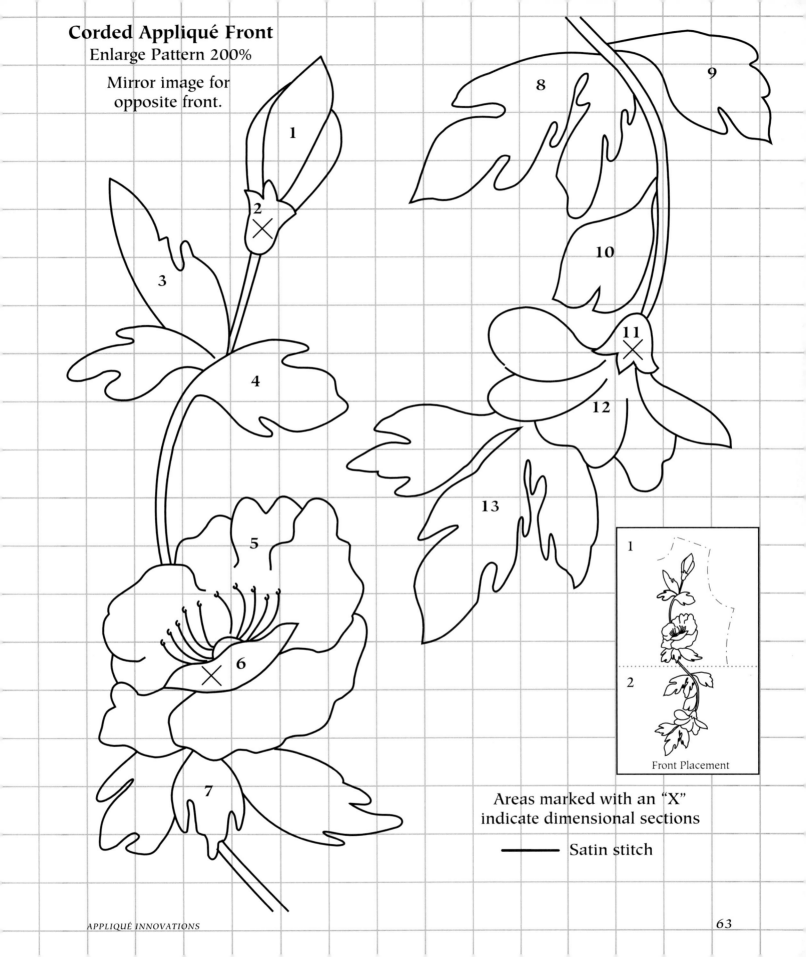

Corded Appliqué Front
Enlarge Pattern 200%

Mirror image for
opposite front.

1

2

3

4

5

6

7

8

9

10

11

12

13

Front Placement

1

2

Areas marked with an "X"
indicate dimensional sections

—— Satin stitch

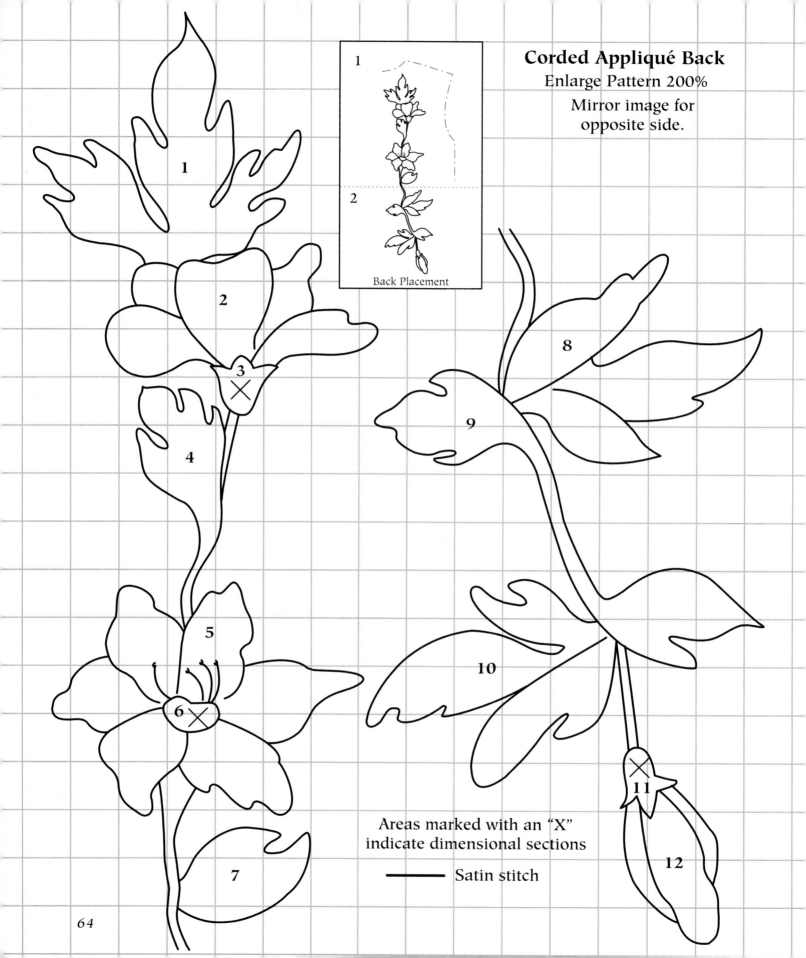

Corded Appliqué Back
Enlarge Pattern 200%
Mirror image for
opposite side.

1

2

Back Placement

1

2

3

4

5

6

7

8

9

10

11

12

Areas marked with an "X"
indicate dimensional sections

— Satin stitch

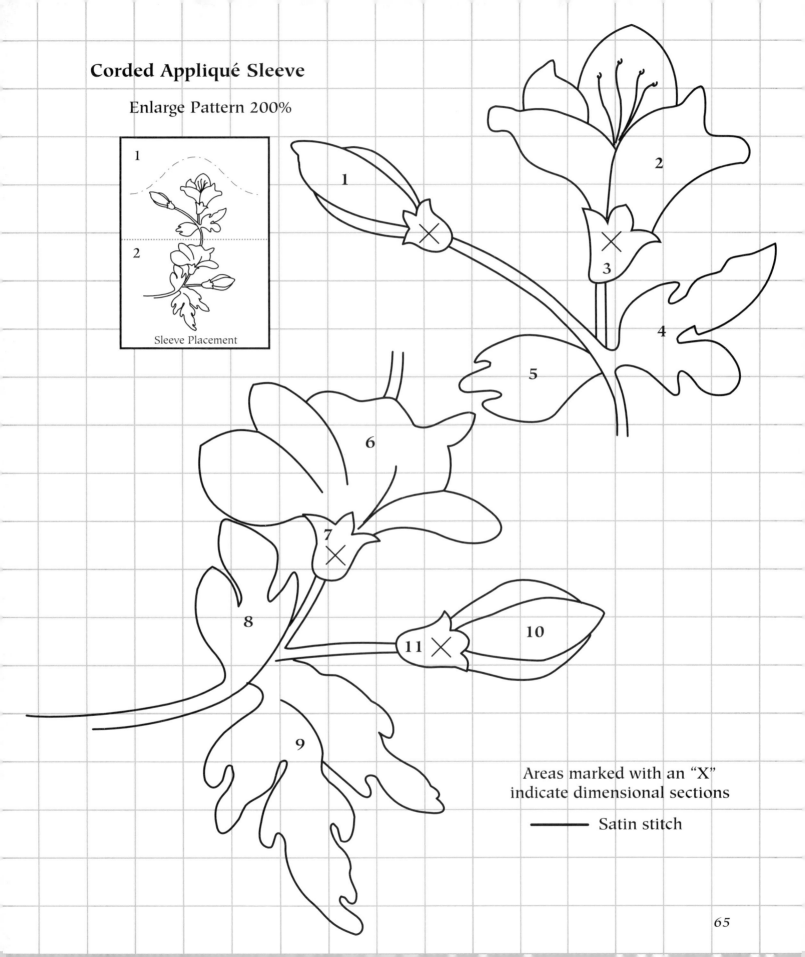

Corded Appliqué Sleeve

Enlarge Pattern 200%

1

2

Sleeve Placement

1

2

3

4

5

6

7

8

9

10

11

Areas marked with an "X"
indicate dimensional sections

—— Satin stitch

65

CUTWORK APPLIQUÉ

Cutwork has traditionally been associated with fine fabrics, such as linens, cottons (batiste and lawn), and a variety of silks. Over the centuries, distinctions have been made between the types of cutwork created depending upon the amount of fabric cut away within the motif designs, along with the type and amount of embroidery stitches used to connect the larger open areas of the motif.

In its simplest form, a minimal amount of fabric is cut away. And since the open areas are relatively small, connecting stitches are not necessary. As the open areas become larger, "bars" of spider-web-type stitches are added. Commonly referred to as "stitching on air," these bars add both strength and beauty to the design.

A contemporary interpretation of this lovely machine art has been applied to this green wool-jersey tunic top. The background cutwork leaves are stitched on a complementary-colored green linen, and the dimensional peach flowers are of the wool jersey. Smaller segments of cutwork motifs also can be used on sleeves, blouse fronts, collars, or yokes.

Materials and Supplies:

- ❖ Wool-jersey yardage as required on pattern for tunic top plus minimum of ½ yard
- ❖ 1 yard linen in matching color
- ❖ 1 yard wool jersey in a complementary color for dimensional flowers
- ❖ 2½ yards paper-backed fusible stabilizer
- ❖ 2 large spools of matching rayon or cotton embroidery thread
- ❖ Fabric marking pens
- ❖ Large embroidery hoop
- ❖ 1 package stabilizer appropriate to fabric selected
- ❖ 1 package water-soluble stabilizer
- ❖ Optional: color-coordinated beads

Appliqué Instructions:

1. Trace the leaf motif on two lengths of fabric adding approximately 3" - 4" to the complete outline. Cut the fabric into rectangles and set aside.

2. Trace two sets of the leaf motif onto paper-backed fusible stabilizer, mirror-imaging one design. Add or subtract motif sections according to your selected pattern size. The front and back leaves should meet at the side seams.

3. Fuse the traced leaf motifs to the wrong side of the linen fabric and trim along the outside edge, leaving ¼" for the side seams as illustrated. **Don't cut out** the center of the leaves yet.

4. Remove the paper and press the linen onto the lower edge of the right side of both jersey tunic pieces, matching the side seams.

5. With a fabric marking pen, draw the leaf motifs again on the right side of the linen. Trim both the linen and wool jersey from the center of the leaves.

6. Place the chosen stabilizer underneath and straight-stitch (stitch length: 2mm) around all cut edges.

7. Wind two or three bobbins with the same thread as used in the needle. Select a zigzag stitch (stitch length: satin stitch and stitch width: 2 mm). Stitch along the outside and inside of the leaf motifs starting with the background leaves first. Stitch the leaves as they would overlap — bottom to top.

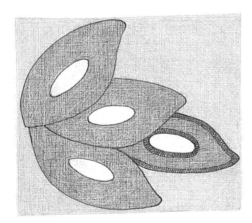

SEWING TIP

Slightly rounded corners, inside and outside, and points in cutwork look nicer and are stronger, and wear better than sharp corners.

8. When approaching the outside corner, stitch until the needle is approximately the width of the stitch from the corner. Taking two to four stitches, "walk" around the corner one stitch at a time. The presser foot lifter and needle-down function are most helpful in this procedure. Repeat this technique for inside corners as well.

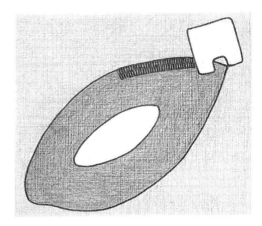

9. Stitch as many leaves as possible without stopping, by straight-stitching between the leaves or "walking" to the next portion of the design. Remove the stabilizer from the back of the fabric.

10. For the dimensional flowers, press the paper-backed fusible stabilizer to the wrong side of one rectangular piece of wool jersey. Remove the paper and fuse this piece to the wrong side of a second rectangle of the same color wool-jersey knit.

11. Trace the flower motif on a clear plastic template and cut out.

12. Using the plastic template and a fabric marking pen, trace approximately 50 - 55 flowers onto the fused fabrics. Cut out all the flowers.

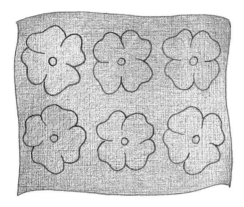

13. Place as many cut flowers as you can between two layers of water-soluble stabilizer. Place the stabilizer and flowers in a hoop.

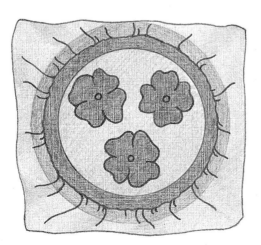

14. Satin-stitch (stitch length: satin stitch and stitch length: 2mm) around all the flower edges. *Note:* To add definition to the petals, straight-stitch along the inside of all satin stitching before or after removing hoop.

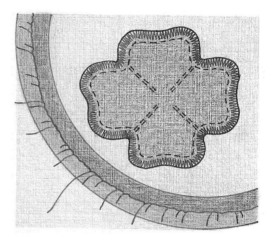

15. Remove the stabilizer and attach the flowers to leaf "intersections" with an eyelet stitch or another similar type of stitch or bartack.

16. Remove the presser foot and lower the feed dogs to add two or three beads to the centers of all the eyelets. Knot the first stitch in the fabric by stitching in place. With the help of Teflon™-tipped beading tweezers,

stitch through the center hole of one bead. Take another knotting stitch on the other side of the bead to secure. Continue attaching the remaining beads.

17. Place the pattern pieces on the two embellished sections and cut out the front and back of your tunic top. Complete the garment according to the pattern instructions.

SEWING TIP

When finishing the side seams, fold up the bottom of the ¼" extension before sewing or serging.

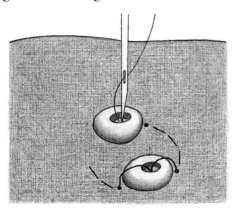

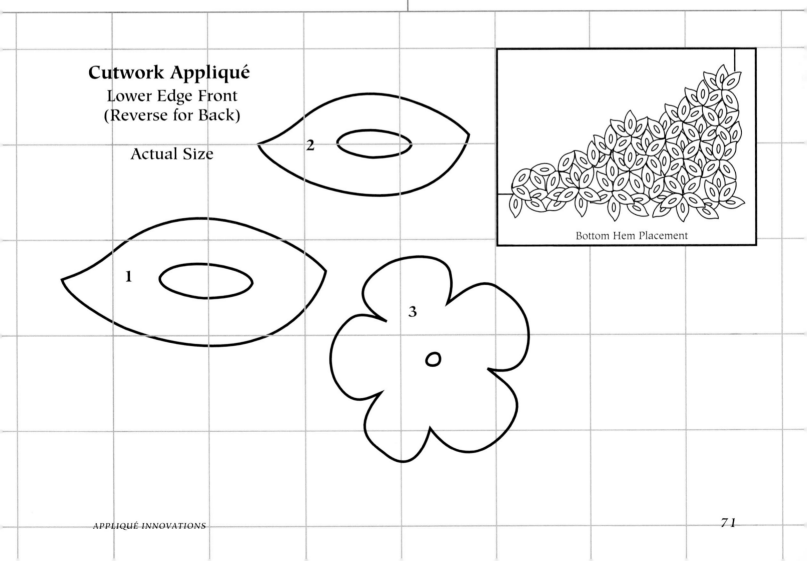

Cutwork Appliqué
Lower Edge Front
(Reverse for Back)

Actual Size

2

1

3

Bottom Hem Placement

ELASTICATIONS

Elastic thread can be used in many different applications, on the bobbin to create yardage for replacing sections of a garment design, such as a bodice, or to create interesting effects for appliqué motifs.

Elastic thread comes in a variety of weights, colors, and stretch characteristics. Choose the elastic thread weight in relation to the decorative fabric weight. The most suitable fabrics vary from the finest and lightest weight to medium-weight fabrics both in woven and knit varieties. Heavier fabrics do not work as well with elastic applications since the project becomes weighted down, bulky, and unattractive.

Fabric weight, the fabric finish, and dyes all play into the amount of shirring that will take place. A good rule to apply when selecting fabric for shirring is to purchase a piece two to four times larger than each pattern piece requires. Testing, therefore, is essential whenever a new fabric is introduced. Do not rely on the settings and the amount of shirring created from previous projects.

The following projects incorporate two different methods of elastication: to complement a dress pattern design and to utilize the same technique in motifs for appliqué.

Test the fabric and a variety of stitches to decide whether you like the elastic shown on the right side or wrong side of the fabric. Choose an interesting colored thread or a metallic to blend or match with your fabric background color or print. Since elastic thread is used in the bobbin, adjust the bobbin case tension slightly to accommodate the thickness. The needle thread will show slightly, so you may choose to blend this thread with the color of the elastic or use a contrasting metallic thread to complement and enhance.

Materials and Supplies:

- ❖ Challis print fabric for child's dress; yardage as required on pattern plus 2 to 3 times more as required for bodice
- ❖ ¼ yard of challis print for appliqués
- ❖ Coordinating fabric for vest as required on pattern, plus ¼ yard for appliqués
- ❖ Coordinating fabric for jacket(s), plus ¼ yard for appliqués
- ❖ ½ yard of matching jacket fabric for purse
- ❖ ¼ yard of 2 to 3 coordinating solid colored fabrics for appliqués
- ❖ 2 yards fusible tricot underlining
- ❖ Standard presser foot or gathering foot for hard-to-gather fabrics
- ❖ Extra bobbin case

Shirring Instructions

1. By-pass the bobbin pre-tension and slowly wind several bobbins by machine with elastic thread. Insert one into the bobbin case and adjust the tension accordingly.

> **SEWING TIP**
>
> **Winding the bobbins slowly on the machine gives a more consistent stretching characteristic than winding by hand.**

2. Use either good-quality all-purpose thread in the needle or a decorative thread of your choice. Stitch the first row across the cross-wise grain of the fabric. Increase the needle tension slowly while stitching to encourage more gathering. If you have reached the maximum tension setting and the fabric is still not gathering sufficiently, you may want to use a gathering foot. Keep in mind that

shrinkage will occur further when you steam the piece after it's completed.

> **SEWING TIP**
>
> **Usually a straight stitch or a narrow zigzag is recommended for creating substantial amounts of yardage. If smaller pieces are needed for the appliqués, bias and curved stitches will produce unusual results, such as the running stitch, blindhem stitch, or other interesting stitches on your machine. In addition, experiment with the stitch width for unique results.**

3. Determine the desired distance between the elasticized rows, evenly or unevenly spaced. Continue stitching across the fabric until the desired amount is gathered, plus a little extra.

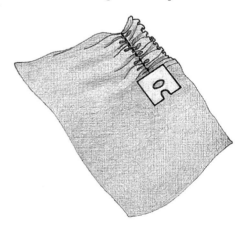

4. Once the yardage has been sewn, set the stitches by steaming completely on both sides of the fabric. Just like magic, it will continue to shrink before your eyes.
5. Underlining the elasticized area is recommended to prevent the garment from becoming stretched or distorted from use or abuse. To minimize any additional weight to this

area, use the finest or sheerest stabilized tricot underlining available. (For example, So Sheer™ is ideal for this application as it maintains the unnatural appearance of the fabric and can be fused at low settings.) Press with light pressure, enough to fuse the underlining to the piece but not enough to flatten the "scrunched" fabric. A Teflon™ press sheet works well for this application.

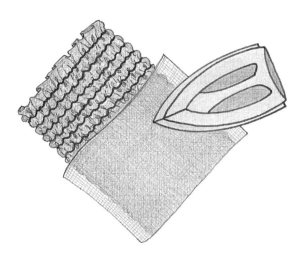

6. Continue constructing the dress according to the pattern instructions, using the underlined elasticized fabric for the bodice section.

Appliqué Instructions:

This technique works well on simply designed motifs. If a more elaborate motif is desired, such as ones with defined curves and corners, then the following step is required.

1. Cut and prepare the border motif pieces using the flower patterns provided and following the Basic Appliqué Instructions, steps 1 through 3, at the beginning of this chapter. Do not stitch the appliqué pieces to the project fabric yet.

2. Following the "bottoms up" method, appliqué the leaves in the traditional manner by first satin stitching the centers and then the entire leaf. Straight-stitch along the inside edge of the satin stitch to highlight the outlines of the leaves.

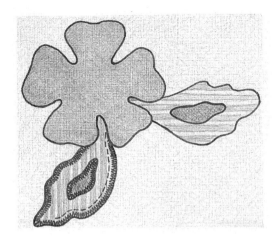

3. Using the reverse appliqué technique, place the elasticized fabric right side to wrong side under the border motif and straight-stitch around the center of the border fabric following the design.

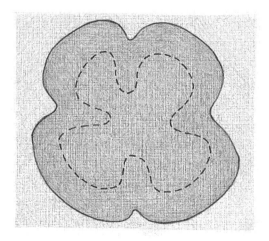

4. Cut away the center section of the flower, being careful not to cut the "scrunched" fabric directly underneath. Trim any excess "scrunched" fabric close to the straight stitching to minimize the bulk.

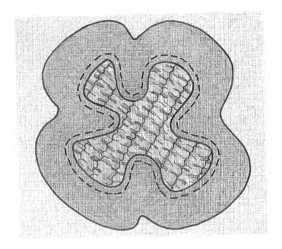

5. Using the straight-stitched lines as a guide, satin-stitch through all layers to finish the raw edges. Continue satin stitching the outer edges to complete the motifs.

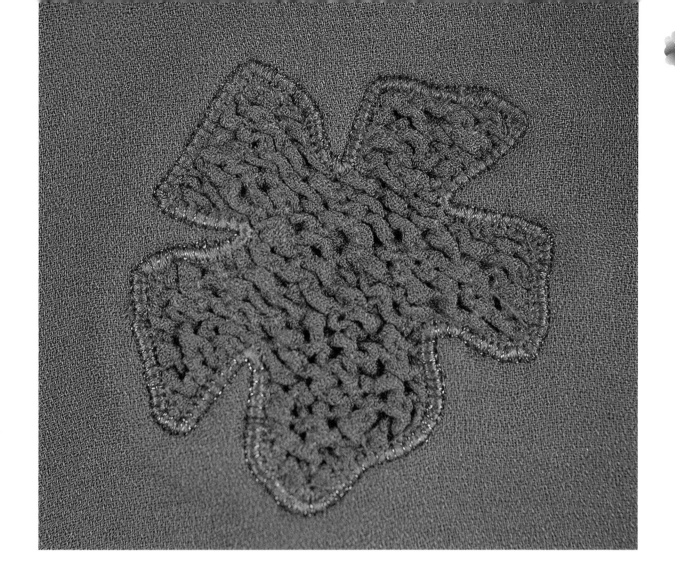

6. Using a metallic or complementary-colored rayon thread and the same width setting, sew a blanket stitch directly over the satin stitch to further highlight the stitch.

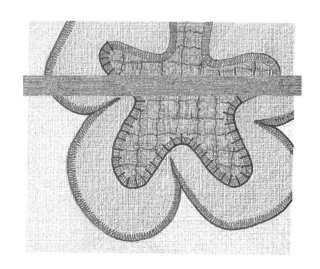

Elastications

Actual Size

Flower A

Flower B

Flower C

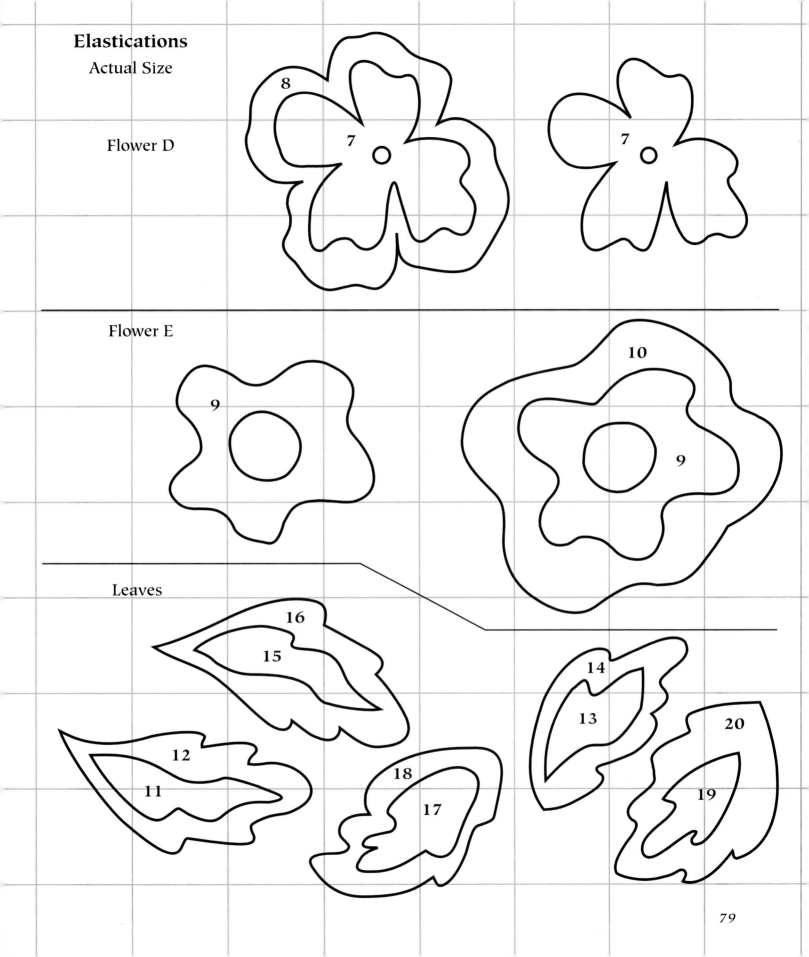

Elastications

Actual Size

Flower D

Flower E

Leaves

79

REVERSE APPLIQUÉ OR NON-TRADITIONAL MOLA APPLIQUÉ

Traditional mola appliqué is an exciting, interesting and colorful technique that incorporates both traditional and reverse appliqué techniques. It is associated with the Indian women of the Kuna (Cuna) tribe living on the San Blas Islands located just off the Atlantic coast of Panama.

Mola is the word referred to by the Kunas as the separate panel which is applied to part of a blouse or is the blouse itself. Worked with great skill, molas are first worked in colorful and intricate-looking panels that are eventually stitched and joined to a simple yoke and sleeves and made into blouses. The panels on the garments are seldom identical. A mola, in general, averages about 15" x 20" in size, making it a comfortable and workable amount of fabric to handle.

Similar to other cultures, traditional molas are inspired by nature itself. You will typically see natural and abstract designs of animals, birds, plants, and sea life, along with designs of the tribe's religious beliefs and life on their islands.

The mola hand-method starts with two to four layers of different colored fabrics placed in an order where parts of the various layers are cut away to reveal a section of the color beneath. The layers are first basted together, and then only small sections of the motif are cut out. After folding under ⅛" along the edge, each area is stitched down with tiny, evenly spaced whip-like stitches. The design emerges as the process of cutting and stitching continues, and extra color is added by pushing small pieces of different colored fabric into the holes of the design. This latter addition of fabric provides more drama, creates illusion and reduces overall bulk. Slits are carefully placed in the design to add color and interest to the background of the piece.

This mola technique is quite interesting when used in a non-traditional way. It is ideal for fashion where unusual interest is desired or where rich bold effects are required. Added as a border around the bottom of a skirt, or used on lapels, pockets of a coat, yokes, collars, and cuffs can be striking. It also can be dramatic on home decorating items such as cushion covers, pillows, and wall hangings.

Materials and Supplies:

❖ Fabric yardage as required on the pattern
❖ 3 - 5¼ yard segments of contrasting colored, closely woven fabrics of 100% cotton, silk or rayon
❖ Paper-backed fusible web
❖ Monofilament thread - clear or dark based on fabric
❖ Decorative threads for added embellishment
❖ Open embroidery foot or leather roller foot

Appliqué Instructions:

1. Trace the outline of the bird motif onto paper-backed fusible web. Draw another line approximately ⅜" outside the first line. Remember to mirror image the design where appropriate when tracing the motifs.

2. Cut the yoke sections using the pattern pieces. Press the traced bird motif, fusible side down, to the wrong side of the top layer of fabric. With fine sharp scissors, cut out the entire motif along the inner line leaving the ⅜" outer edge in place.

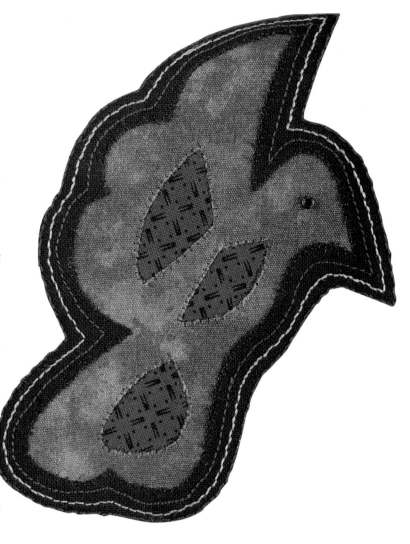

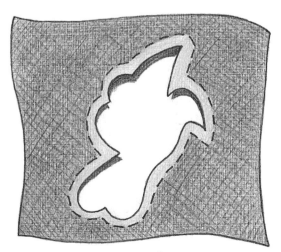

Wrong side

> ### SEWING TIP
>
> Fabric color choice is up to you. Layer your fabrics in a different order until you find which is the best combination. By starting with a dark color for the first layer, contrasting colors will be easier to work with.

3. Trace the motif again, including the ⅜" seam allowance on the paper-backed fusible web. Fuse to the wrong side of the second layer of fabric. Trim away the center design areas and along the ⅜" outer line.

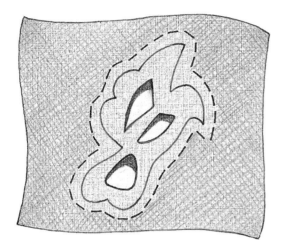

4. Remove the paper backing from the top layer, and with right side to wrong side, center and fuse the second layer to the first under the motif opening.

5. Remove the paper backing from the back of the second layer. With right side to wrong side, fuse a bottom layer of fabric that's large enough to cover the cut-away area to the second layer.

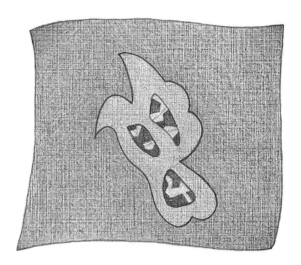

6. With monofilament thread, stitch through all layers using the blanket stitch (stitch length: 1½ - 2 mm and stitch width: ½ - 1 mm) around all the cut-away areas. Fine-tune the stitch settings as required. Alternate stitch choices are a zigzag or blindhem stitch.

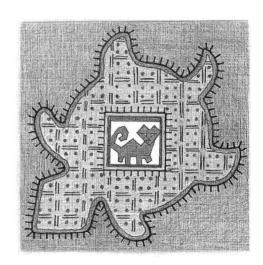

Before cutting, spray the fabrics with sizing to minimize fraying along the edges and/or use a slight amount of non-staining seam sealant on the cut edges before pressing. Let dry completely before handling.

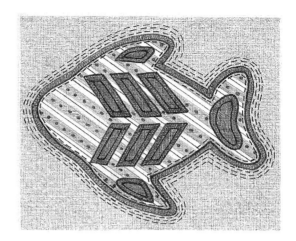

7. For the other motifs, follow the above steps, layering the fabrics in order.
Fish: Stitch the mouth with a multi-motion straight stitch.
Turtle: Satin-stitch (stitch width: 1½ mm) around the inner opening instead of using the blanket stitch.

8. To add beads for eyes on all motifs, remove the presser foot, lower the feed dogs, and stitch in and out of the bead two or three times, "knotting" the stitch before and after each bead.

9. Straight-stitch around each motif with two or three rows of stitching and contrasting threads.

10. Complete the garment construction following the pattern directions.

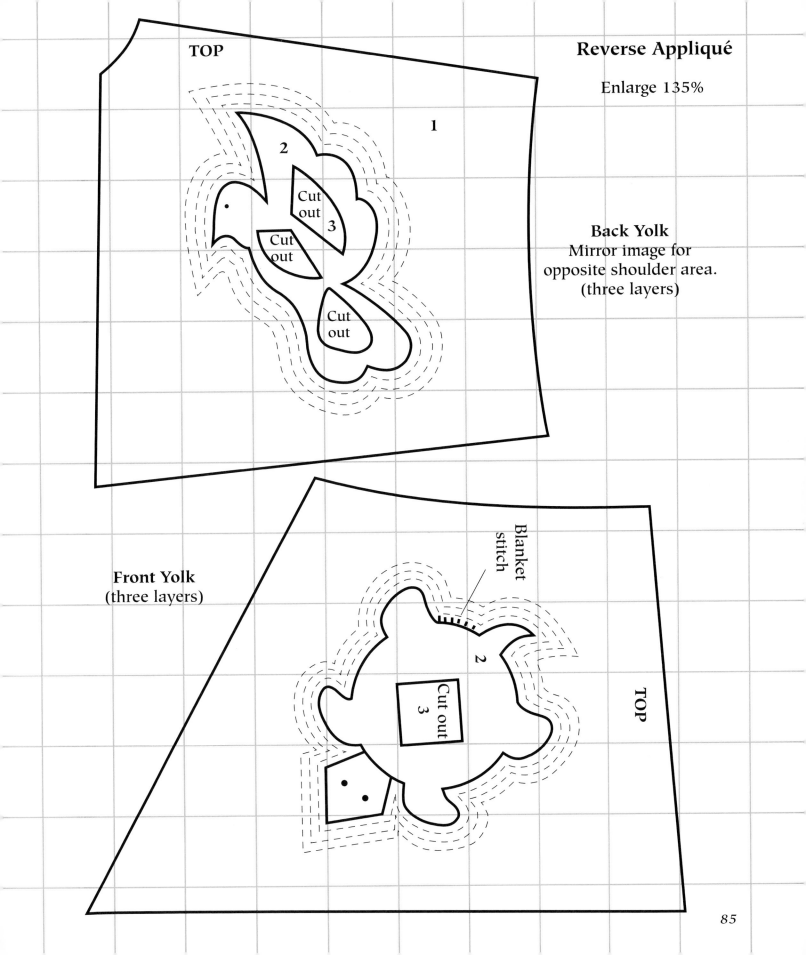

TOP

Reverse Appliqué

Enlarge 135%

1

2

Cut out

3

Cut out

Cut out

Back Yolk
Mirror image for
opposite shoulder area.
(three layers)

Front Yolk
(three layers)

Blanket
stitch

2

Cut out
3

TOP

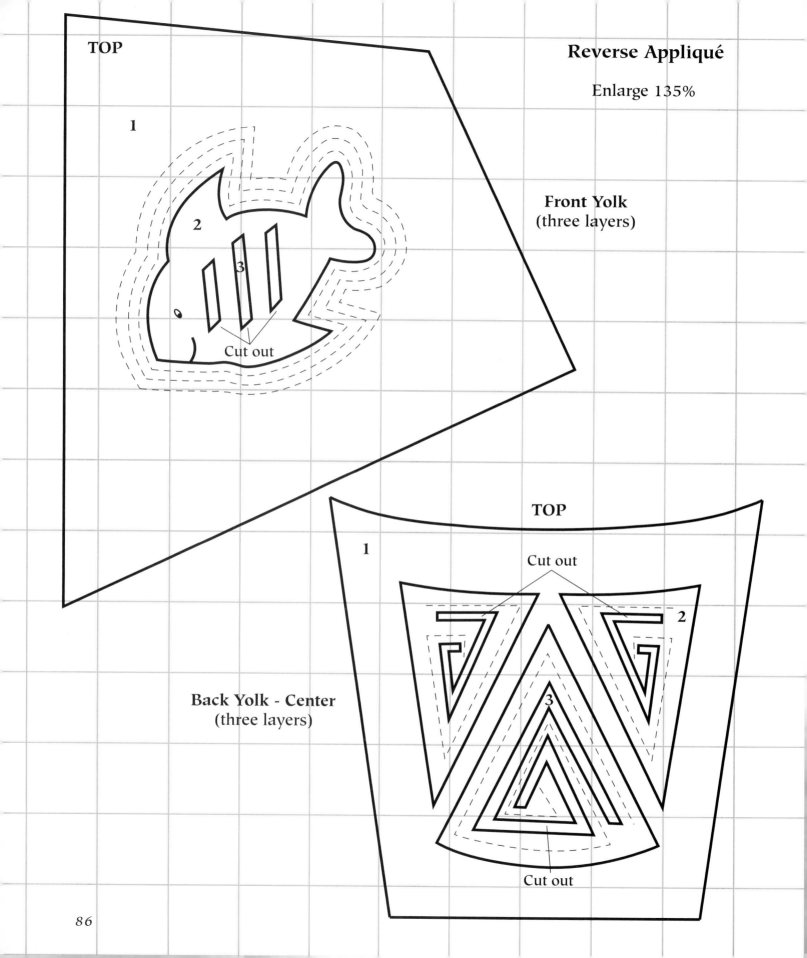

TOP

Reverse Appliqué

Enlarge 135%

1

Front Yolk
(three layers)

2

3

Cut out

TOP

1

Cut out

2

3

Back Yolk - Center
(three layers)

Cut out

SHEER ELEGANCE APPLIQUÉ

A basic or classic blouse or tunic of a simple design lends itself nicely to beautiful, heirloom-type embellishment. With an artful arrangement of roses and leaves on a cotton netting and linen background, the garment takes on an elegant look. Self-fabric linen motifs are used both as a background on the linen and as foreground on the cotton netting. The blouse can be worn over a camisole or a sleeveless blouse, and treated as a "jacket."

Cottons, linens, silks, and blended fibers are suitable base fabrics for this sheer appliqué technique. Along with 100% cotton netting, sheer organza, bridal tulle (two layers), or a fine stretch Lycra netting, which works well with knits, are all appropriate for the sheer.

Materials and Supplies:

❖ Linen, cotton, silk or fabric of choice for blouse; yardage as required on pattern
❖ 2 yards of cotton netting
❖ #30 rayon embroidery thread
❖ #60 cotton bobbin thread
❖ Cording for couching
❖ Tapestry needle or ribbon threader
❖ Ribbon floss
❖ Tear-away stabilizer
❖ Paper-backed fusible web
❖ Fabric marking pen
❖ Open embroidery foot
❖ Standard embroidery foot
❖ Embroidery needles - #80
❖ Double-wing needle - #100
❖ Single-wing needle - #100
❖ Seed pearls

Appliqué Instructions:

1. Cut the front and back sections of the blouse from the linen fabric. Draw an outline of the background netting areas for the

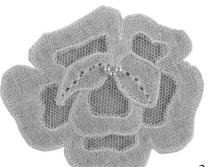

front and back sections onto tear-away stabilizer. Place the tear-away stabilizer under the linen fabric and trace the design on the linen using a fabric marking pen.

2. Cut the netting to fit these areas allowing an extra 2" around all the edges. Place the netting on the wrong side of the linen.

3. Straight-stitch along the drawn design area on the linen. Remove the drawn lines before pressing.

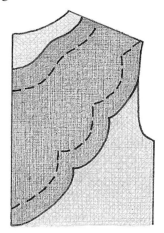

Wrong side

4. With small appliqué scissors, **carefully** cut away the linen from the top of the netting close to the straight stitching line.

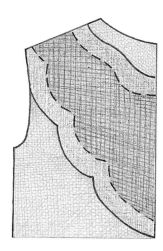

5. Baste one or two layers of stabilizer behind the cotton netting and linen areas before embellishing.

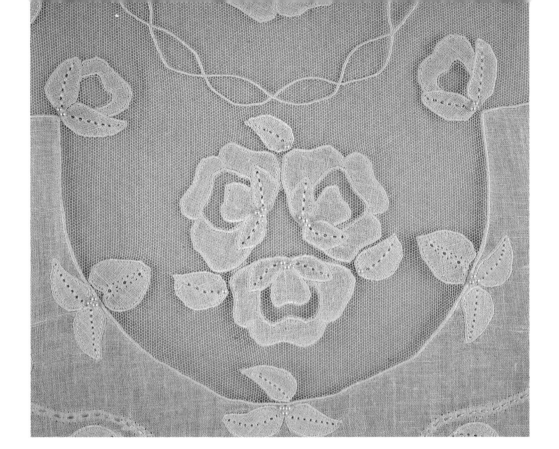

6. Using the standard embroidery foot, couch narrow cord directly over straight-stitched areas with a narrow zigzag stitch (stitch length: 1½mm and stitch width: 1½ - 2mm).

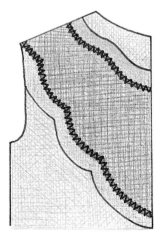

7. Satin-stitch over the cord (stitch length: satin stitch and stitch width: 1½ - 2mm).

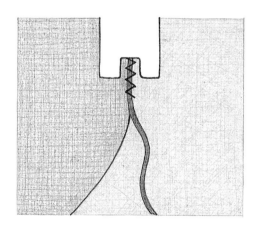

8. Prepare all rose, rosebud, and leaf motifs following the Basic Appliqué Instructions, steps 1 through 4, at the beginning of this chapter. Fuse in place a pleasing arrangement on both the front and back sections, and the collar and cuff areas using the pattern given here.

9. With the marking pen, draw the major connecting vines on the linen. Using a double-wing needle, stitch two rows of straight stitches approximately 3mm in length following the lines. Stitch the first row, turn the fabric in the opposite direction, and stitch the second row so the wing needle re-enters the holes made by the previous row of stitching. This will prepare the fabric for hand-weaving of the ribbon floss.

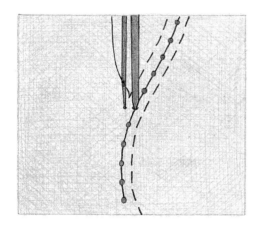

10. Thread a tapestry needle or ribbon threader with ribbon floss. Thread the floss through each pronounced hole.

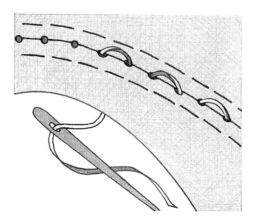

11. On the netting, sew a straight stitch scallop in two rows creating the cable pattern. Using your standard embroidery foot, couch fine cord over the cable design using the two-step process as described in steps 6 and 7.

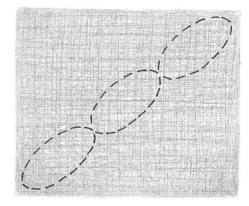

12. Satin-stitch all appliqué motifs in place with a fine zigzag stitch (stitch length: satin stitch and stitch width: no wider than 2mm).
13. With the single wing needle, stitch the centers of the rosebuds using a multi-motion straight stitch.

14. Machine- or hand-stitch pearls on some of the leaf motifs for embellishment.
15. Remove the tear-away stabilizer and trim the netting at the yoke areas close to the satin stitching. Complete the pattern according to the instructions.

Sheer Elegance Right Back, Upper

Mirror image for opposite side.

Enlarge Pattern 200%

Areas marked with an "＊"
indicate a daisy stitch

· · · · · · · Double wing needle

– – – Multi-motion stitch

——— Satin Stitch

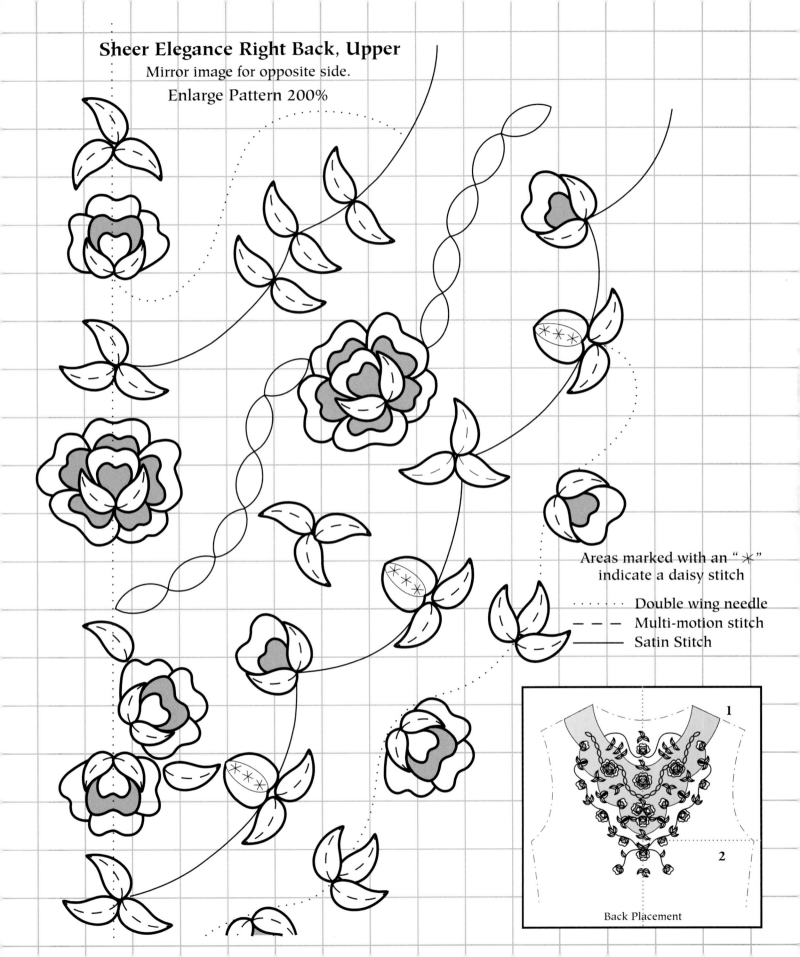

1

2

Back Placement

Sheer Elegance Right Back, Lower
Mirror image for opposite side.
Enlarge Pattern 200%

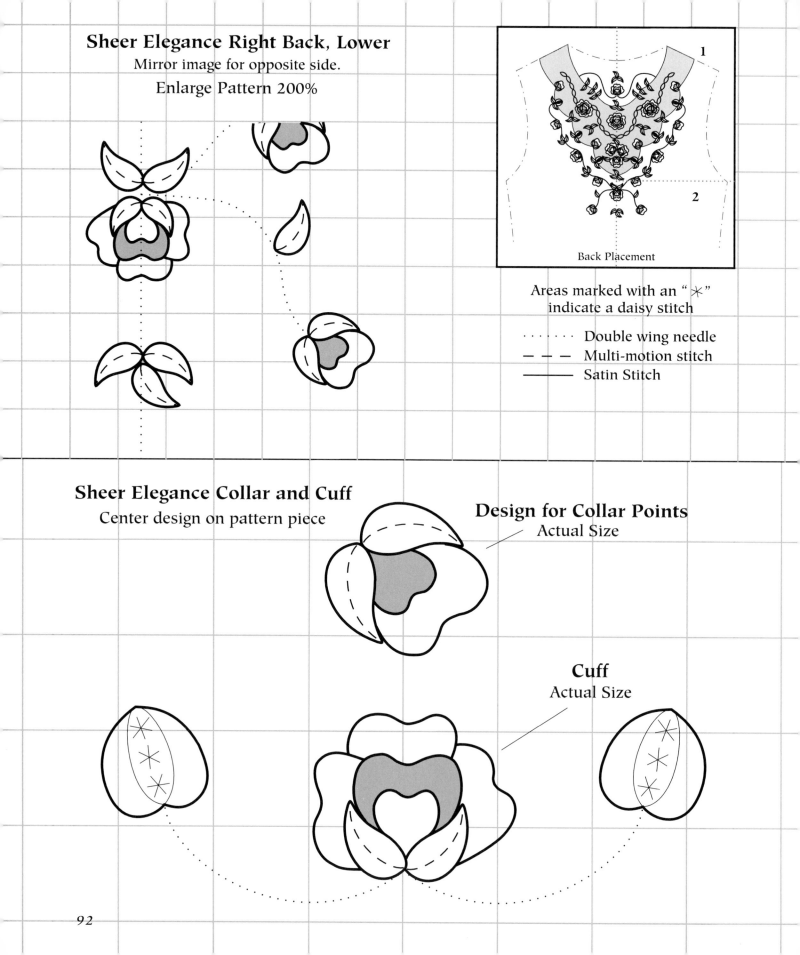

Back Placement

Areas marked with an "✳" indicate a daisy stitch

· · · · · · Double wing needle
– – – Multi-motion stitch
——— Satin Stitch

Sheer Elegance Collar and Cuff
Center design on pattern piece

Design for Collar Points
Actual Size

Cuff
Actual Size

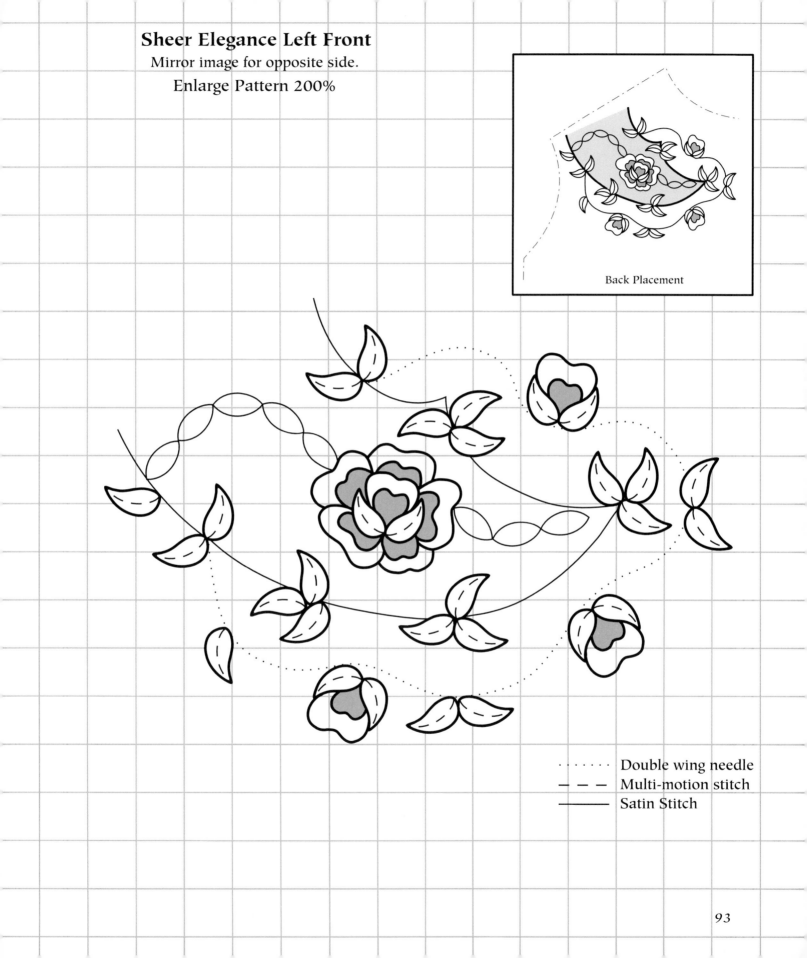

Sheer Elegance Left Front
Mirror image for opposite side.
Enlarge Pattern 200%

Back Placement

· · · · · Double wing needle
– – – Multi-motion stitch
——— Satin Stitch

TONE-ON-TONE APPLIQUÉ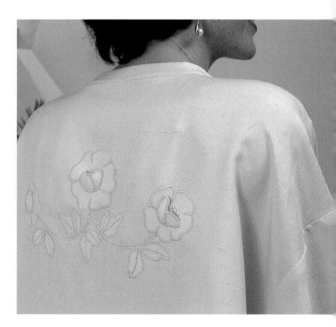

One of the simplest and most elegant forms of appliqué is merely using the same fabric for both the garment and the motif, particularly if the fabric is a luxurious quality. Cutting the motifs on the bias allows just enough differentiation from the straight-of-grain of the garment to highlight this subtle embellishment. The silk douppioni fabric used for this tunic suggests this elegant quality. The simplicity of the motifs used here, which also were used for the "Sheer Elegance" appliqué technique, can be adapted for any of the other appliqué techniques in this book.

Materials and Supplies:

- Silk douppioni fabric; yardage as required on the pattern plus ¼ yard for appliqués
- #30 rayon embroidery thread color-coordinated to fabric
- Tapestry needle or ribbon threader
- Ribbon floss color-coordinated to fabric
- Tear-away stabilizer
- Paper-backed fusible web

- Fabric marking pen
- Open embroidery foot or standard embroidery foot
- Embroidery needles - #80
- Double-wing needle - #100
- Single-wing needle - #100
- Optional: seed pearls

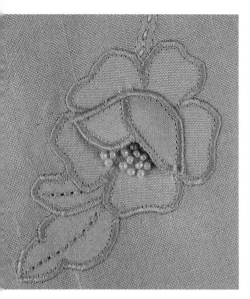

Appliqué Instructions:

1. Prepare the motifs provided for you according to the Basic Appliqué Instructions, steps 1 through 4, described at the beginning of this chapter.

2. Using the double-wing needle, connect the rose and leaf design areas with a straight stitch. Stitch the first row, turn the fabric in the opposite direction, and stitch the second row so the wind needle re-enters the holes made by the previous row of stitching. This prepares the fabric for hand-weaving of the ribbon floss.

3. With the tapestry needle, hand-weave the ribbon floss through the line of holes created by the stitching.

4. Appliqué the flowers and leaves to the background fabric in the traditional manner using a narrow zigzag stitch (stitch length: satin stitch and stitch width: 2mm).

5. Using a single-wing needle, stitch the centers of the leaves with a multi-motion stitch.

6. For a three-dimensional effect, satin-stitch the outer edge of the center flower piece onto a piece of stabilizer.

7. Remove the stabilizer and complete the satin stitching on the flower motif, positioning it to appear as a forward petal.

8. Machine- or hand-stitch seed pearls to each appliquéd flower for embellishment.

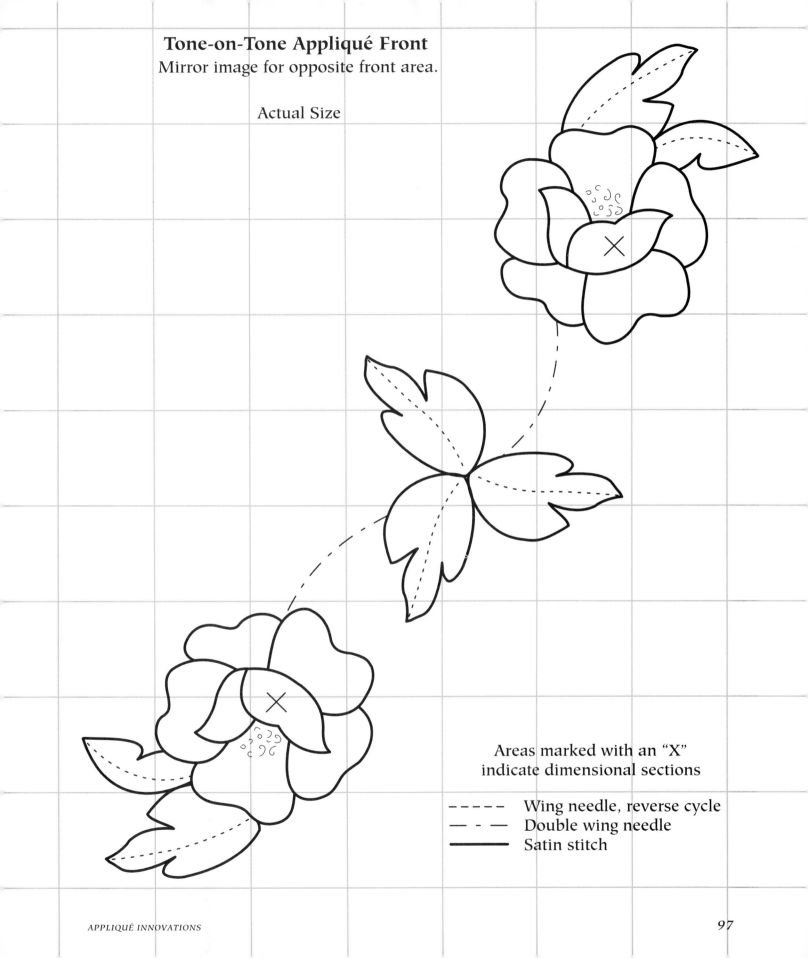

Tone-on-Tone Appliqué Front
Mirror image for opposite front area.

Actual Size

Areas marked with an "X"
indicate dimensional sections

----- Wing needle, reverse cycle
— · — Double wing needle
——— Satin stitch

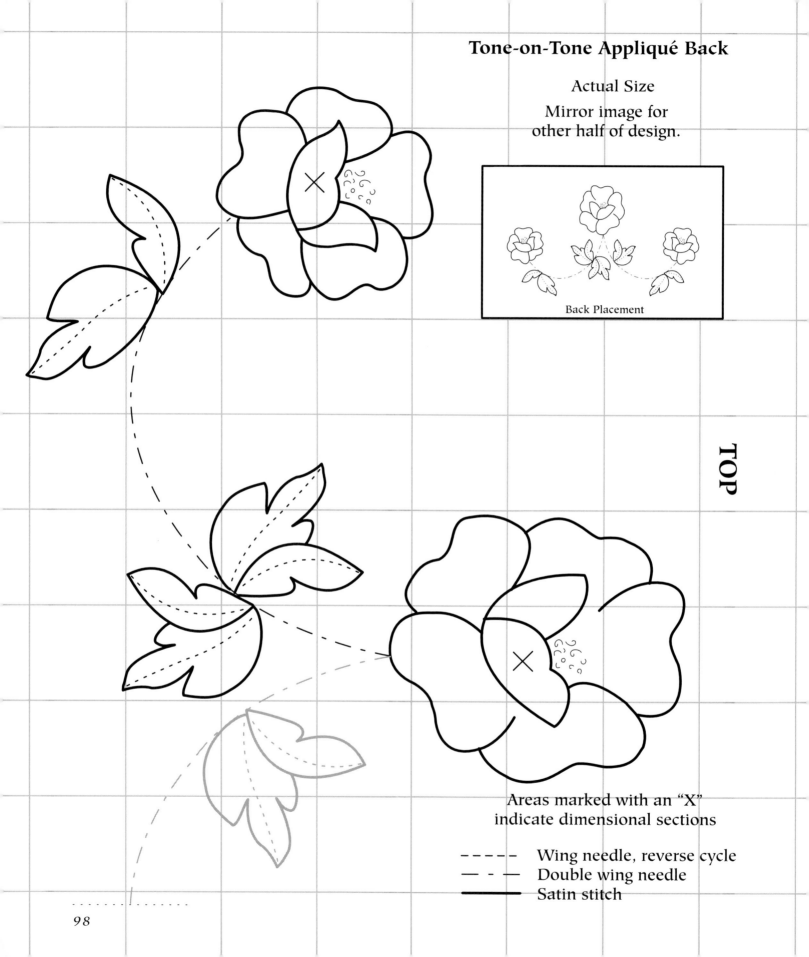

Tone-on-Tone Appliqué Back

Actual Size

Mirror image for
other half of design.

Back Placement

TOP

Areas marked with an "X"
indicate dimensional sections

- - - - -   Wing needle, reverse cycle
— - — -   Double wing needle
————   Satin stitch

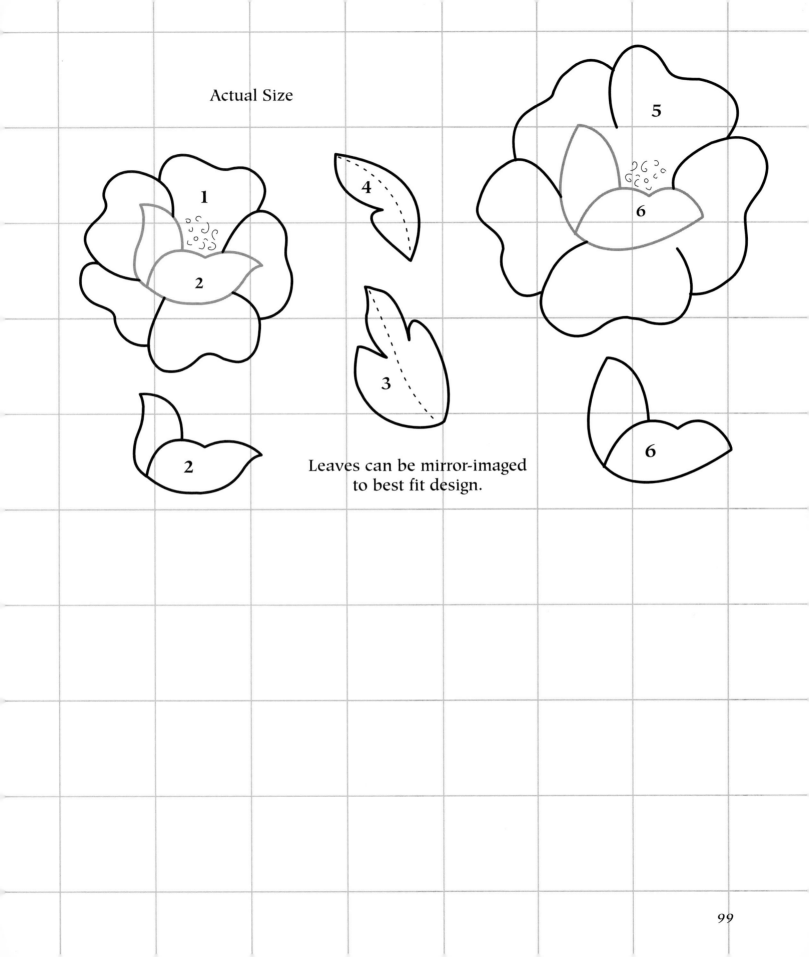

Actual Size

1

2

4

3

2

Leaves can be mirror-imaged
to best fit design.

5

6

6

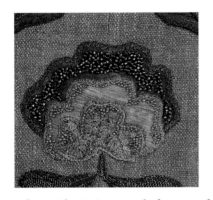

Upside-down appliqué is a non-traditional approach to finishing edges of motifs. It is novel, fun, and an unusual decorative treatment on garments as well as home decorating items. The motifs may be simple or elaborate, and the technique is appropriate for all levels of sewing expertise. In addition, further expansion of this technique includes adding traditional satin stitch and other embroidery stitches. "Thread fabric" is created for textural interest in the appliqués on this garment. Threads unraveled from the fabric itself are used when matching currently available decorative threads is not possible. These threads also provide a blend to the "thread fabric." Embellishments, such as beads, couched cords, threads, and serger trims, display the versatility of this appliqué technique, allowing you to personalize any mood or design interpretation.

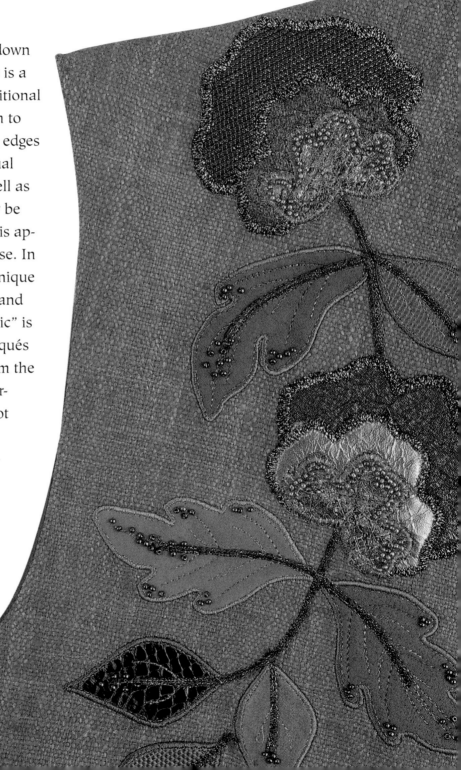

Materials and Supplies:

- ❖ Silk and rayon fabric for jacket and skirt; yardage as required on pattern plus 1 yard for over-vest
- ❖ 3 - 5¼ yard pieces of lizard or snake skins, synthetic or natural suede, metallic fabric, and "thread fabric"
- ❖ Fusible tricot interfacing
- ❖ Burn-away stabilizer
- ❖ Thick rayon, cotton and metallic-type threads for serger
- ❖ 6-strand cotton embroidery floss
- ❖ 4-strand rayon and silk floss
- ❖ Ribbon floss
- ❖ "Fabric threads" (not to be confused with "thread fabric")
- ❖ Extra bobbin case
- ❖ Open embroidery feet - standard and Teflon™
- ❖ Couching feet
- ❖ Variety of embroidery, topstitching, and metallic needles
- ❖ Fine glass beads in coordinating colors
- ❖ 2 - 7" zippers
- ❖ 1 - 9" zipper
- ❖ Optional: Leather roller foot

Appliqué Instructions:

1. Prepare the appliqué motifs according to the Basic Appliqué Instructions at the beginning of this chapter. Underline any metallic fabrics on the wrong side with a fine tricot fusible interfacing. This will support and stabilize the metallic fibers.

SEWING TIP

Since most decorative threads are fragile, particularly the metallics, use a Teflon™ press sheet for this application. Fabric press cloths will not always protect the threads from the hot iron surface. The Teflon™ press sheet also protects fragile fabrics such as synthetic and natural suedes and skins.

2. Position and mark placement of the motifs on the jacket and vest, fronts and backs.
3. From the right side, accurately straight stitch or zigzag using a very narrow width (stitch length: 1.5mm, stitch width: 1 - 1.5 mm) along the edge of the large flower motifs.

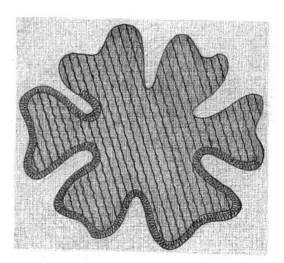

4. Place a heavy decorative thread in the extra bobbin case, fine tune the length, width, and test the tension on a scrap of fabric. Thicker threads require less tension and slightly longer stitch lengths as the zigzag fills in quickly.

5. On the wrong side of the garment, zigzag to cover the previous stitching line with the decorative bobbin thread.

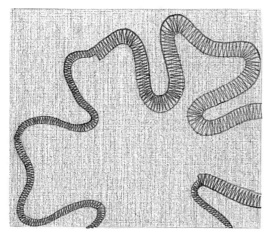

Wrong side

SEWING TIP

Remember which side will be used as the right side of the appliqué motif when changing from needle thread to bobbin thread stitching.

6. From the right side, straight-stitch along outer edge of bobbin stitching with a matching metallic thread for more definition.

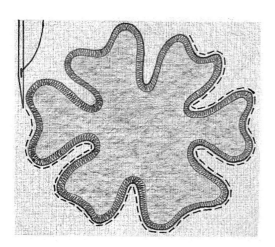

7. Create the inner part of the flower from "thread fabric." "Thread Fabric" is made by simply straight stitching in a random manner onto a 10" × 10" piece of burn-away stabilizer. A combination of bobbin threads and needle threads are stitched to create a texture similar to a fine fabric. The more random the stitching the more interesting the texture. When sufficient stitching is completed, the stabilizer is "burned-away" by using a hot iron and following the manufacturer's instructions.

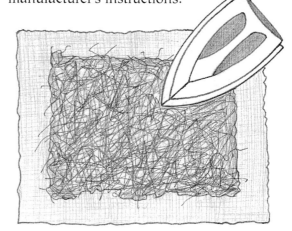

8. Cut the inner flower motif from the "thread fabric." From the right side, satin-stitch (stitch length: satin stitch and stitch width: 2mm) this piece over the previously stitched motif using rayon thread.

9. Over-stitch the satin stitch with an open stitch, such as the buttonhole stitch, using a fine metallic thread and the same stitch width, for added dimension.

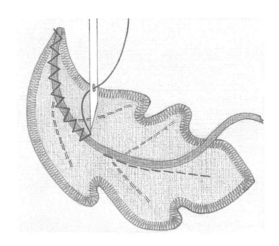

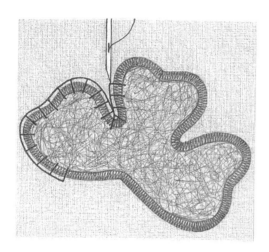

10. Cut the leaf motifs from a variety of natural or synthetic suedes, lizard or snake skins. On the right side and using rayon thread, satin stitch (stitch length: satin stitch and stitch width: 1½ - 2mm) the leaf edges next to the flower motif.

11. Straight-stitch outside the stitching line with a fine metallic thread.

12. Emphasize the leaf, main vein and stem, by either satin stitching over cord or by making serger trim and couching it in place. Smaller veins may be straight-stitched, alternating rayon and metallic threads.

13. Continue to prepare the flower motifs according to the instructions above. Additional layers of fabric can be added to each flower as was done on the jacket back.

SEWING TIP

Clear plastic templates aid in designing motif arrangements of flowers and leaves. First, trace the templates on paper to see which arrangements are more appealing.

14. The sleeve motifs use only one layer of the "thread fabric." Cut and attach the motif following the instructions in step 8.

15. The background stitching around the flower simulates an appliqué effect. With decorative threads of heavy rayon, cotton, and metallic on the bobbin, alternate single rows of straight stitching outlining the flower motif.

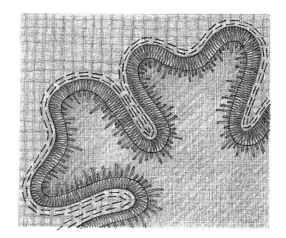

16. Add vines and leaves by straight stitching with heavy threads in the bobbin. From the right side, stitch with fine metallic thread along the side of the heavy bobbin-stitched vines for more texture and color.

17. Fine glass beads have been added to highlight parts of the flowers and leaves. Attach by hand or machine.

The Over-Vest

Make an over-vest addition giving the jacket two different appliqué variations. After the jacket has been completed, measure down the front and back to cover the already finished appliqués. Transfer these measurements to the jacket pattern pieces. (You may have to cut the over-vest one size larger than the jacket pattern for wearing ease.) Cut lining pieces using the same new pattern pieces.

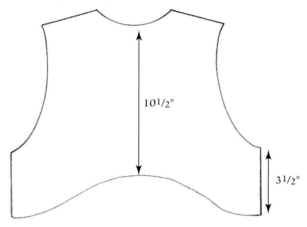

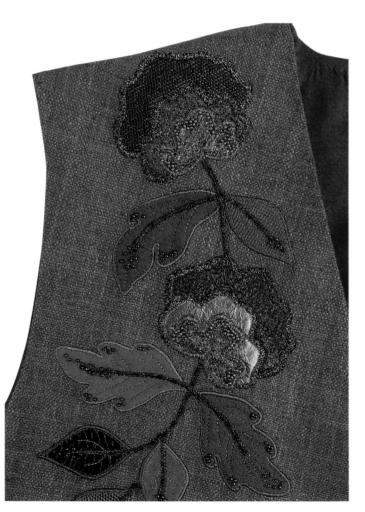

The motifs on the front and back of the over-vest are other ways to arrange the basic motifs. The same stitching procedures and techniques are used as described above. The over-vest is another way of giving added life to the jacket. Another option is to make a simple, unadorned jacket and embellish the over-vest to get further use of the jacket itself.

Purse

Add a complimentary purse with appliquéed motifs to finish the outfit. The motifs are appliquéd in the same manner as on the jacket. Cut two lining pieces the same size as the outer purse pieces.

After the embellishment has been completed on the right sides, insert the zippers into each piece according to the pattern piece. Baste a lining piece each to the front and back fabric embellished pieces. Handle the two layers as one when inserting the zipper into end of the purse. Stitch along the remaining three sides attaching the shoulder cord at dots. Pull through zipper end to right side. This will allow a separate pocket area for both front and back zippers.

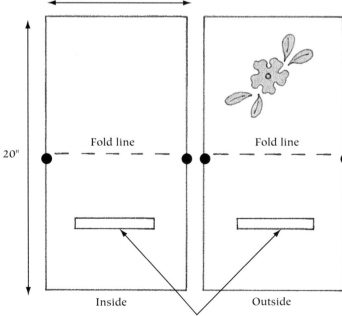

10¼"

20"

Fold line   Fold line

(½" Seam allowance)

Inside   Outside

Zippers

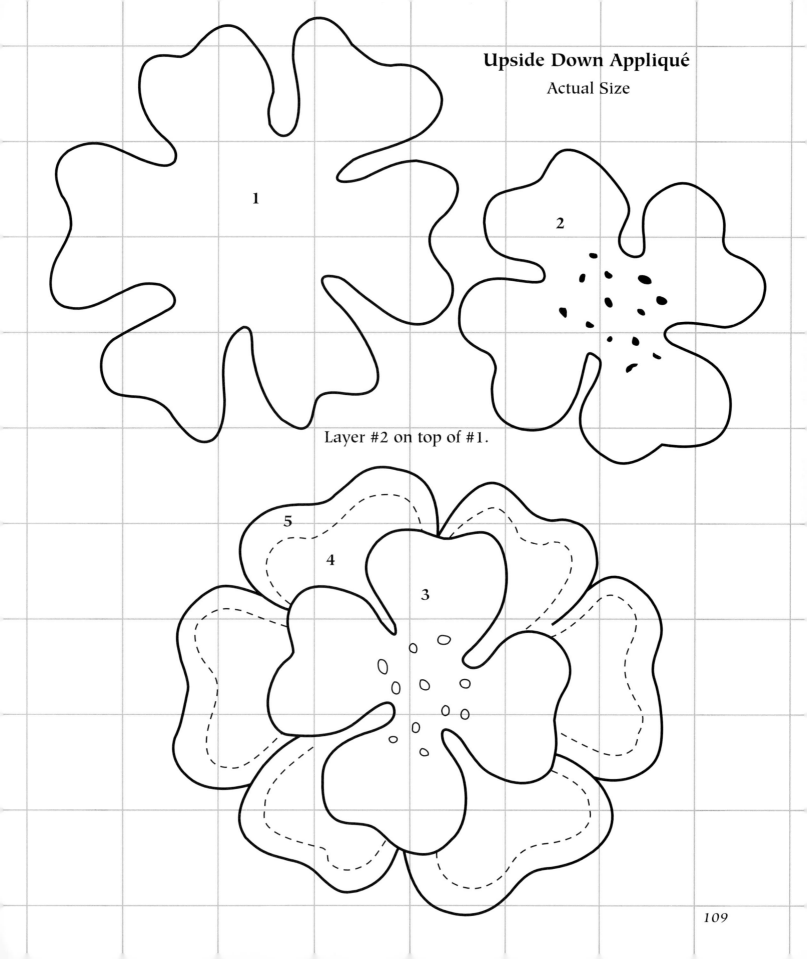

Upside Down Appliqué

Actual Size

1

2

Layer #2 on top of #1.

5

4

3

109

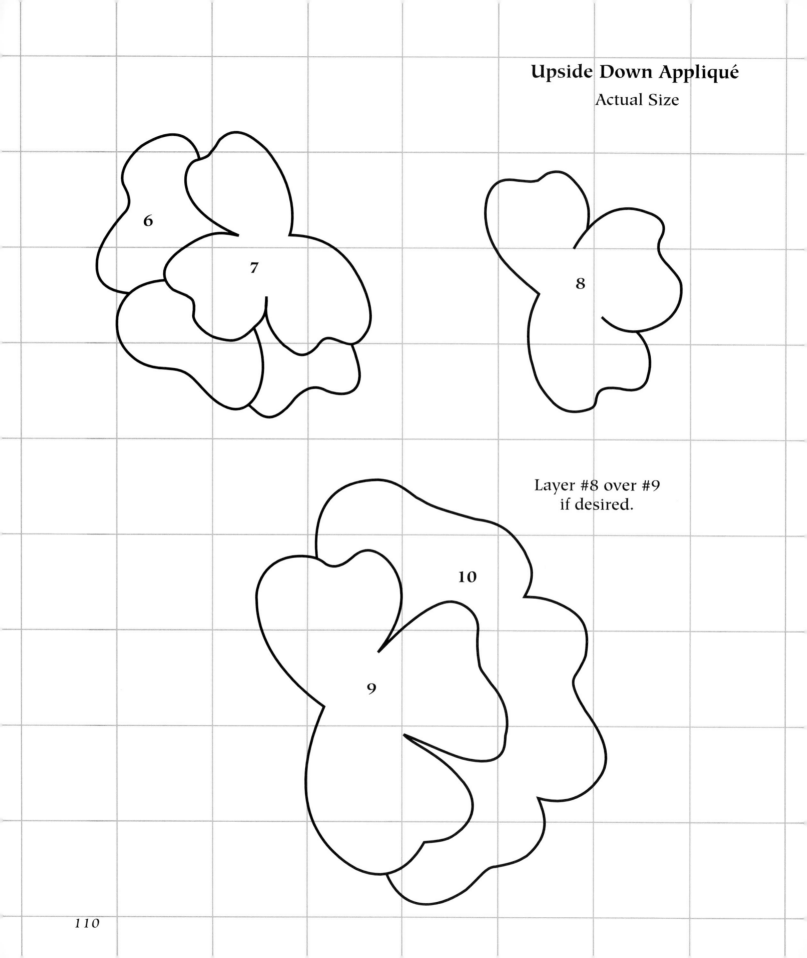

Upside Down Appliqué
Actual Size

6

7

8

Layer #8 over #9
if desired.

10

9

Upside Down Appliqué
Actual Size

11

13

12

15

14

16

18

17

—— Satin Stitch
Stitch veins with heavy threads

WOOL APPLIQUÉ

There are several creative ways to use this appliqué-tion providing beautiful results on a variety of fabrics. Wool is a natural fabric and easy to work with, though you can achieve marvelous variations and wonderful results on many other fabrics including synthetics. Fabric weight also is an important factor, as medium- to heavier-weight fabrics create the best results.

The secret for this technique lies in the threads used. Though there are several companies that make a similar product, the thread used is made of a soft wool and acrylic blend. Found most often in a 2-ply version, this thread can be stitched from the top with a #90 or #100 topstitch or embroidery needle. A thicker version also is available but it can only be used on the bobbin or on the looper of an overlock machine. Since this thread is thicker than most embroidery threads, it covers more area in the stitch length and width, and therefore the satin stitch fills in quicker. Take this fact into consideration when planning the motif design along with the your actual stitch length and width.

Unlike the lightweight bobbin thread traditionally used in appliqué, good stitch quality is easier to achieve with a heavier bobbin thread, such as all-purpose thread used for normal sewing. Long staple polyester or 100% cotton threads work nicely. A light or dark bobbin thread is sufficient, though a complementary shade as used in the needle may be preferable.

Thread your machine with the 2-ply "yarn" on top and the bobbin thread of choice. Select a wide satin stitch and test your tension, beginning with a balanced setting, as for normal sewing. Tighten the needle tension slightly if the thread appears too loose. Continue to tighten until none of the bobbin thread shows.

Materials and Supplies:

❖ Wool fabric yardage as required on pattern for young girl's coat with detachable capelet, beret, and muff

❖ 3 - 5¼ yard pieces of complementary colored fabric for motifs

❖ 2-ply wool/acrylic thread in coordinating colors

❖ All-purpose thread for bobbin

❖ Embroidery or topstitching needles - #90 or #100

❖ Metallic threads in coordinating colors

❖ Open embroidery foot

❖ Water-soluble stabilizer

❖ Tapestry needle

Appliqué Instructions:

1. Trace and cut out the appliqué motifs according to the Basic Appliqué Instructions, steps 1 through 4, given at the beginning of this chapter

2. The leaf and flower motifs are handled in two different ways. The leaves are considered "background" embellishments. In the first step, fuse leaf motifs to background fabric as described in the Basic Appliqué Instructions, step 3.

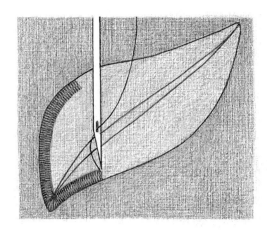

5. Over-stitch the finished leaves with a blanket stitch and metallic thread using the same stitch width. This stitch is added to enhance the motif and not to overpower the original stitching. When approaching more difficult curves and points, lower the feed dogs and select "Pattern Begin," if available on your machine. Manipulate the curves and points during the straight stitch portion of the stitch.

3. Straight-stitch (stitch length: 3mm) the center vein lines as indicated on the pattern pieces.

4. Satin-stitch (stitch length: satin stitch and stitch width: 3mm) the leaf edges using the wool/acrylic needle thread.

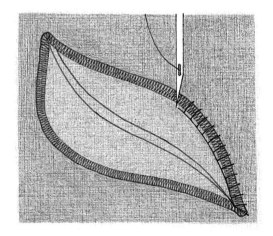

6. For the beret and collar, trace the flower motifs onto paper-backed fusible web. Press the traced motifs onto the motif fabric, cut out the motif and remove the paper.

7. Sandwich the motif between two layers of water-soluble stabilizer and place in the appropriate size hoop.

SEWING TIP

Have a variety of hoop sizes ready with motifs in position to save time when sewing.

8. Satin-stitch (stitch length: satin stitch and stitch width: 3.0mm) around the edges. The stitching is done through the top layer of stabilizer with an open embroidery foot. Or try lowering the feed dogs and stitching the edge using a free-motion application.

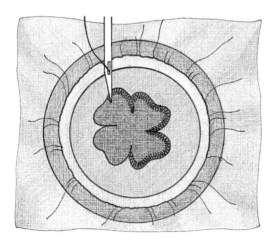

9. Once all the motifs are completed, remove the stabilizer following the manufacturers instructions. Straight-stitch (stitch length: 2mm) the motif onto the garment fabric next to the satin stitch with metallic thread. This extra line of stitching adds a dimensional appearance to the flower edges.

10. For the motifs on the muff, after completing steps 6 through 9, place the second layer of the flower motif on top and straight-stitch onto the base.

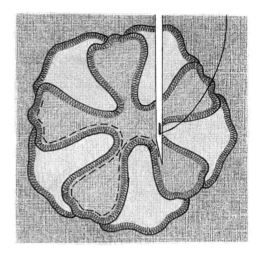

11. For the capelet front, trace and apply the complete flower motif following the Basic Appliqué Instructions, steps 1 through 3.

12. Zigzag with the widest satin stitch your machine can stitch on the rows of lines indicated.

13. Along one edge of the wide satin stitch, stitch a narrow satin stitch (stitch length: 1.5mm). Complete each row following this two-step procedure, shading thread colors in one- or two- row progressions.

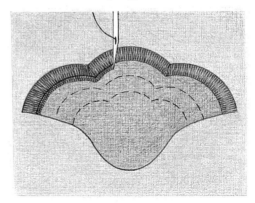

14. When all the rows are completed, using a pair of very sharp embroidery scissors, cut the bobbin thread of the wide satin stitch close to, but not through, the second row of narrow zigzag stitches.

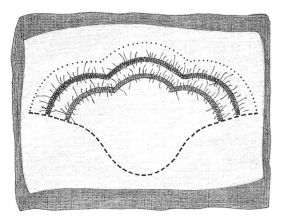

Wrong side

15. From the right side, lift the satin stitch away from the edge with a tapestry needle creating the fringe.

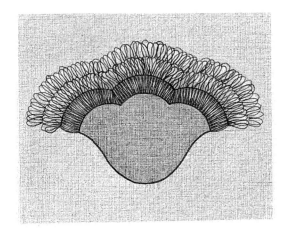

16. Satin-stitch the flower base to the motif according to steps 4 and 5 above.

17. On the capelet back, four different flower motifs are used. Stitch the first flower according to steps 11 through 16.

18. For the second and third flowers, trace and stitch two complete layers as previously described in steps 6 through 9.

19. Use a built-in straight-stitch eyelet (if available on your machine), or draw and stitch a small straight-stitch circle in the flower centers.

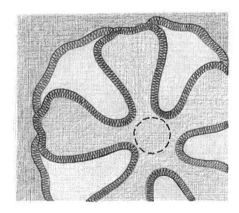

20. Using this straight-stitched circle as your guide, satin-stitch with the widest width around the circle. Complete the fringe in the flower centers in the same manner as on the above flowers.

21. For the fourth flower motif, trace the center of the motif onto the garment fabric. Starting with the widest satin-stitch width, stitch rows next to each other filling in the design. Reduce the stitch width by 0.5 - 1mm each time a new row is started.

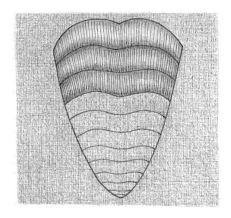

22. Straight-stitch with metallic thread between each row.

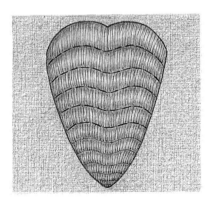

23. Add the outer layer, following steps 7 through 9.

24. To create the cable designs on the sleeves and the front and back pleats of the coat under the removable capelet, use a straight-stitch scallop (stitch length: 2.5 - 3mm and stitch width: 5 - 9mm) and form the cable.

25. Couch premade serger trim or purchased cord with a buttonhole stitch following the cable design.

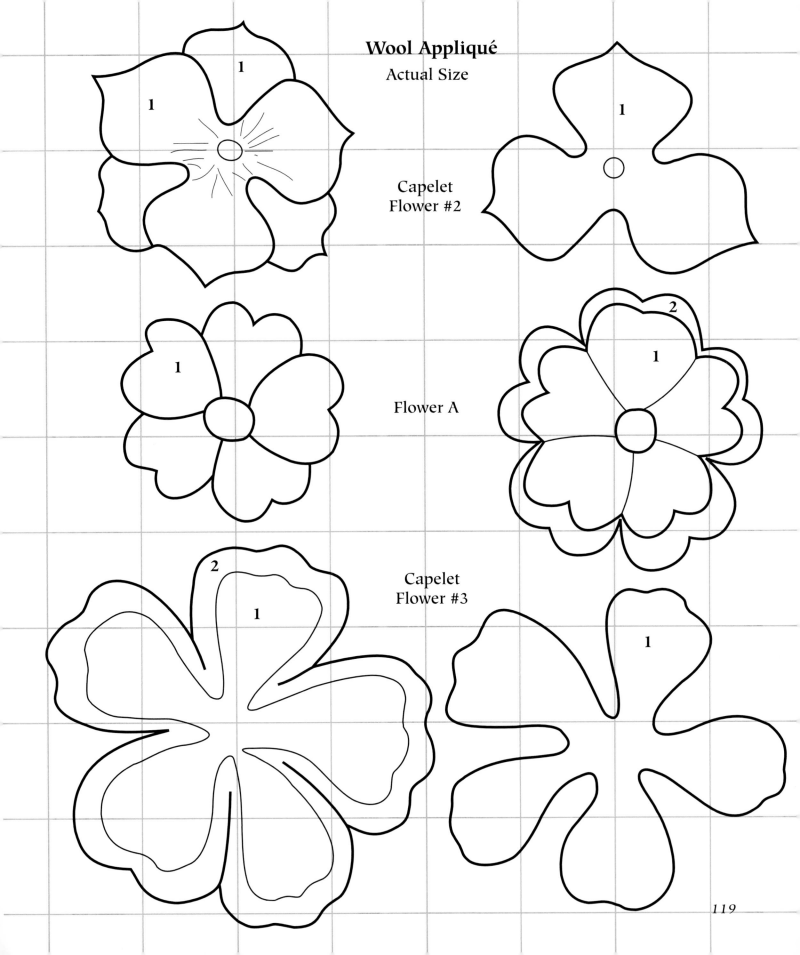

Wool Appliqué
Actual Size

Capelet
Flower #2

Flower A

Capelet
Flower #3

119

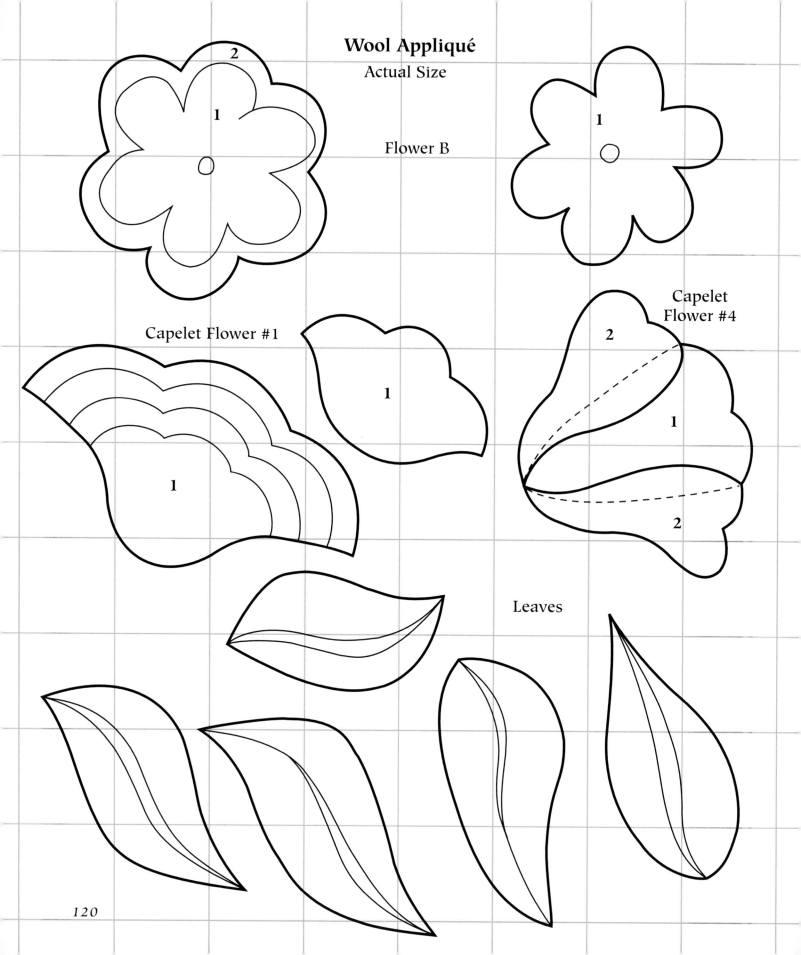

Wool Appliqué
Actual Size

Flower B

2

1

1

Capelet Flower #1

1

1

1

Capelet
Flower #4

2

1

2

Leaves

Wool Appliqué

Enlarge 135%

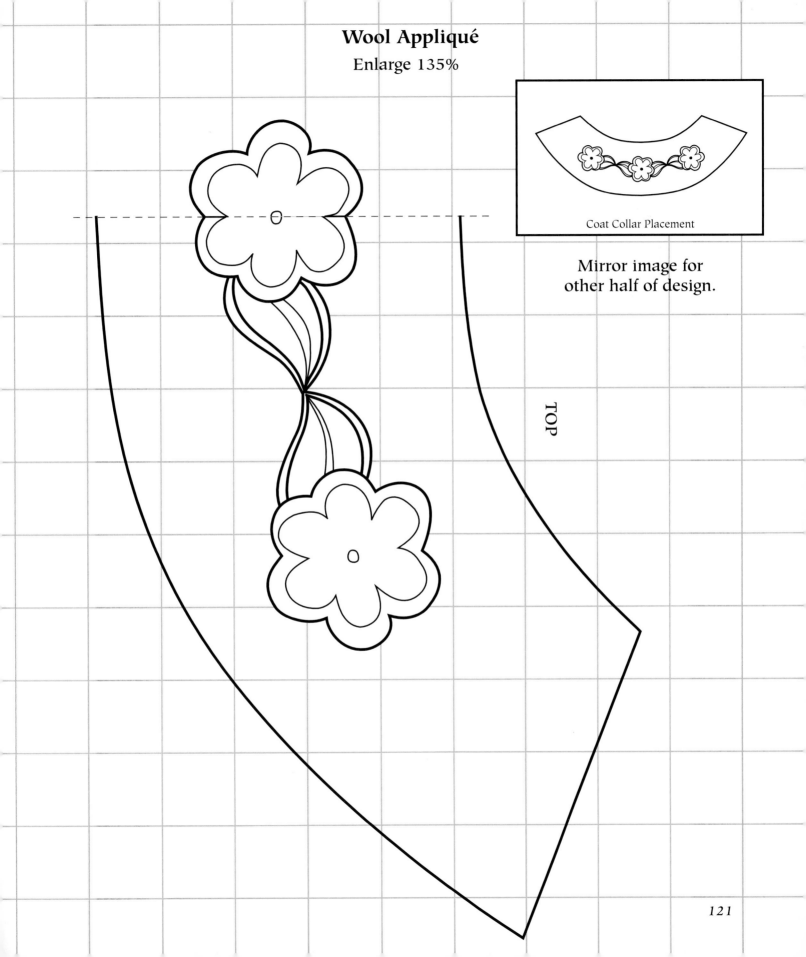

Coat Collar Placement

Mirror image for
other half of design.

TOP

Metric Equivalents

INCHES TO MILLIMETERS AND CENTIMETERS
MM—millimeters   CM—centimeters

Inches	MM	CM	Inches	CM	Inches	CM
⅛	3	0.3	9	22.9	30	76.2
¼	6	0.6	10	25.4	31	78.7
⅜	10	1.0	11	27.9	32	81.3
½	13	1.3	12	30.5	33	83.8
⅝	16	1.6	13	33.0	34	86.4
¾	19	1.9	14	35.6	35	88.9
⅞	22	2.2	15	38.1	36	91.4
1	25	2.5	16	40.6	37	94.0
1¼	32	3.2	17	43.2	38	96.5
1½	38	3.8	18	45.7	39	99.1
1¾	44	4.4	19	48.3	40	101.6
2	51	5.1	20	50.8	41	104.1
2½	64	6.4	21	53.3	42	106.7
3	76	7.6	22	55.9	43	109.2
3½	89	8.9	23	58.4	44	111.8
4	102	10.2	24	61.0	45	114.3
4½	114	11.4	25	63.5	46	116.8
5	127	12.7	26	66.0	47	119.4
6	152	15.2	27	68.6	48	121.9
7	178	17.8	28	71.1	49	124.5
8	203	20.3	29	73.7	50	127.0

METRIC CONVERSION CHART

Yards	Inches	Meters
⅛	4.5	0.11
¼	9	0.23
⅜	13.5	0.34
½	18	0.46
⅝	22.5	0.57
¾	27	0.69
⅞	31.5	0.80
1	36	0.91
1⅛	40.5	1.03
1¼	45	1.14
1⅜	49.5	1.26
1½	54	1.37
1⅝	58.5	1.49
1¾	63	1.60
1⅞	67.5	1.71
2	72	1.83

Index

ABOUT THE AUTHOR

Agnes Mercik holds degrees in both Business and Fashion Design and has an extensive sewing and serging background. She has written several books on sewing and serging, and contributes to several national and international sewing and craft publications.

Her love affair with sewing began in early childhood and, by the age of 14, she was designing costumes for her own dance studio. This interest in sewing continued throughout her professional dance and modeling career. Today, Agnes continues to share her expertise and enthusiasm for sewing by teaching a variety of sewing and serging classes; providing new product information and education to retailers and their employees; and by participating in consumer programs, such as quilt symposiums, Home Economic workshops, and national sewing seminars.

Agnes continues to research and write on a variety of sewing machine and serger techniques, create class outlines, and design patterns using innovative sewing and serging techniques. She was the main writer and technician for the *Advanced Serger Guide and Supplement* for Bernina of America. Her designs for Bernina-Vogue patterns were used in national ads and consumer programs. In 1991, she received "The Outstanding Sewing Specialist" award and a trip to Hong Kong from Bernina of America.

She has contributed to *New Creative Serging Illustrated* by Pati Palmer, Gail Brown and Sue Green; *The Complete Book of Machine Quilting* by Robbie and Tony Fanning; Vogue & Butterick's *Craft Projects*; *The Experts' Book of Sewing Tips & Techniques* from Rodale; and *The Ultimate Serger Answer Guide* by Gail Brown, Naomi Baker, and Cindy Kacynski.